SEPARATION FROM THE WORLD
FOR AMERICAN PEACE CHURCHES:
ASSET OR HANDICAP?

The front cover illustrations of Anne Austin and of Mary Dyer are taken, by kind permission, from details at the foot of a Quaker Tapestry panel headed 'Mary Fisher'. This is one of 77 panels of the internationally famous Quaker Tapestry which can be seen in Kendal's historic Friends Meeting House, in Cumbria, England.

Mary Dyer, depicted at the right, after reprieve and banishment, felt a spiritual compulsion to return. She was therefore hanged on Boston Common, Massachusetts, where her statue now stands (see text pages 1 to 6).

This book by eminent scholars from several countries is the outcome of a workshop at the Luxembourg conference of the European Association for American Studies in 1994. It is also a practical 'fruit' of a recent active, international organization called Quakers Uniting in Publications (QUIP), stemming from the three of their annual conferences held so far in England, at the Quaker conference centres of Jordans Hostel, Charney Manor and Woodbrooke College, attended by Professor Louis and the undersigned.

Trustees are grateful for supporting grants from Orléans Université in France and from the European Association for American Studies towards the cost of this publication.

WILLIAM K. SESSIONS
Chairman Sessions Book Trust
December 1996

Contents

Foreword

by Professor Jeanne Henriette Louis

In 1994 the European Association for American Studies held its biennial conference in Luxemburg on the topic: 'The Insular Dream: Obsession and Resistance'. The theme had been suggested by my colleague at the University of Orléans, Prof. Bernard Vincent with the following introduction:

> When in January 1776 Tom Paine explained how preposterous it was for a continent to be governed by an island, he forgot to say that the American continent itself was to a large extent surrounded with water, and he also failed to see that the insular dream, i.e. the dream of political and cultural isolationism, was to become, so to speak, a constant variable of the American dream- and that this would remain true all along, from George Washington's Farewell Address to Pat Buchanan's recent rejection of any American involvement in European and Third World Affairs.
>
> U.S. diplomacy, economy, education, art, culture, ways of thinking and writing and creating have all, at one time, or another, been affected by the temptation of isolation, isolationism, parochialism, self-sufficiency, and other forms of imperviousness to, or ignorance of, external distant, foreign influences.
>
> Against the ever-present background of the American quest for identity, this insular and sometimes almost autistic obsession has naturally met, over the years and centuries, with various forms of criticism and resistance, both inside and outside the United States.
>
> It should be added that the American dream of isolationism has sometimes been ambiguously shared by non-Americans, if only through such conflicting 'cris du coeur' as 'U.S. Go Home' and 'Thanks for the Marshall Plan'.

We could also add that the United States are not a continent, but only part of a continent, but the debate on intervention in the world or isolation from the rest of the world is still very relevant for this nation in 1996.

In 1994 I felt inspired by this general theme, and was struck by the fact that the insular dream is also a religious theme. It recurs in the motivations of immigrants to North America in the colonial period. Isolation was connected with immigration: isolating oneself from Europe in order to live in a new world, often for religious reasons. But separation from the world is a particularly recurrent theme with *historic peace churches*, sometimes considered as actors of the *Radical reformation*: mainly Mennonites, Quakers, Brethren and Moravians. And then 'the world' means 'society', or Gentiles: those who do not belong to the group.

I was prompted to offer a workshop on the theme: 'Separation from the World as an Incentive or Obstacle to Creativity for Historic Peace Churches?' and was fortunate when Professor Louis Billington, from Hull University, accepted to coordinate the potential workshop with me. Three colleagues responded: Frédéric Limare, Emma Marras and Frederic Fransen. This was enough for the workshop to take place. It did take place, and in his report on the workshop, Louis Billington wrote: 'Discussion was lively, especially in the Monday session when colleagues from a wide variety of disciplines brought new perspectives on the subject'.[1]

For Christians, to be, or not to be part of the world, is an old question. Monks in the Catholic Church have decided that separation from the world makes it easier to obey God's principles. The Protestant reformation considered monastic life as artificial, but some actors of the *Radical reformation* decided in favor of symbolical lines of separation, such as dress, or way of life. The separation may be partly geographical, (and so it was for immigrants from Europe to North America) but it may also be conventional.

An interesting study on the topic was made by Amish writer William R. McGrath in his booklet *Separation Throughout Church History*. McGrath speaks (or writes) for separation from the world. He relies on the Bible to advocate such practices, and makes a difference between 'harlot churches' and 'faithful churches' (meaning *peace churches*). He states that the primitive Christian church was faithful to God and refused to conform to the world. Conformity to the world started with Emperor Constantine, and faithfulness was substantially restored by the Anabaptist movement in the 16th century, McGrath writes.[2] In the booklet *1,000 Questions and Answers on points of Christian doctrine*, Daniel Kauffman has a chapter on nonconformity to the world. One of the biblical references he gives for it is Rom.12:2, 'Be not conformed to this world'.[3]

The Amish and the Friends (or Quakers) are probably at the two ends of the spectrum where separation from the world is concerned. Between them stand the Mennonites (wherefrom the Amish movement was born in 1693 in Sainte-Marie-aux-Mines, in Alsace) and the Moravians, among other groups. When the Quaker William Penn founded Pennsylvania in 1682, the groups that were going to be called later *historic peace churches* considered Pennsylvania as a haven, and saw the Province as a privileged land of immigration in North America.William Penn and the Quakers who founded Pennsylvania with him, somehow challenged the principle of separation from the world by setting up a Quaker government. They took the risk of playing into politics. The Mennonites who settled down in Pennsylvania at the turn of the 17th and 18th centuries became mainly farmers. They went as far as voting for Quakers at election time, but they did not run for political responsibilities for themselves. The Amish, who came to Pennsylvania from 1737 onwards, did not even vote, but they would rather be in Pennsylvania than anywhere else. After the Holy Experiment in Pennsylvania ended (1756), Friends no longer governed the Province. They became marginal again, getting closer to Mennonites in this regard. When the United States were born, Quakers and Mennonites were consistent in their separation from the world in that most of them refused to fight in the United States' wars, and this is why, together with Brethren, they came to be recognized as *historic peace churches* in the 20th century.

The following articles examine some aspects of the issue of separation from the world within three *peace churches*: Quakers, Mennonites and Moravians. It would not be easy to follow a chronological order to present them, for chronology is different whether we refer to the birth of movements in Europe or to the time of their immigration to the United States. If we take into account the European origins of the Moravian group, in the 15th century, Moravians are first. But they only emigrated to North America in the 18th century. Likewise, the Mennonite movement was born in continental Europe in the 16th century, but the first Mennonite immigrants to North America only came a few years after the first Quakers (second half of the 17th century). Whereas the Quaker movement, or Religious Society of Friends was born on the British isles in the second half of the seventeenth century, but the first Friends reached the American continent no later than 1756. So, we shall not follow any chronological order to present these articles, but rather what appears as 'common sense' order: the first two articles deal with Quakers in North America in the colonial period and the 19th century. Frédéric Limare stresses that separation from the mainstream of American Christianity was forced upon Friends, and concludes that marginality was beneficial to creativity. Jeanne Henriette Louis focuses her study on microscopic Nantucket island in the 18th and 19th centuries. The island became predominantly Quaker in the 18th century, then Quakerism went stale in the following century. The study of an island is a privilege for such a theme as the insular dream. Separation from the continent may be seen as separation from 'the world'. But the very fact that Quakerism was dominant on the island together with material gains derived from whaling, created a Quaker oligarchy in the 19th century, and killed the creativity in the long run. Not to end on a depressing note, one should add that a small creative Quaker group is being revived on Nantucket island nowadays, which proves that even staleness must no more be taken for granted than creativity.

There, one question already arises: is not creativity bound to end the isolation that fostered it? And then, when the relations with the world take place, whose values win? The problem is a permanent one. In the case of Nantucket, the world's values eventually stifled the creativity born out of isolation.

The question of relations between identity and playing into politics is eventually raised by Frederic Fransen in his article 'Uneasy Citizens: An Essay on the Difficulties in Creating a Mennonite Politics'. Frederic Fransen sees the Mennonite separation from the world as fostering a political naivety which weakened their admirable attempts to draw on their peace traditions challenging America's military adventures in Vietnam and the Gulf. But he does not think that Mennonite specificity could survive an end to isolation.

The last (but not least) article deals with Moravians. In her well documented study, Emma Marras, who is an Alumni of Salem College, sees Moravian isolation as a creative force enabling the *Unitas Fratrum* to develop musical traditions and educational institutions. Salem College in Winston Salem now wants to go beyond parochialism and become an international college, and successfully responds to this challenge. We could be tempted to say that Moravians were more successful than Quakers and Mennonites in blending creativity and reconciliation with the world, saving their identity and abolishing fences at the same time. Things are not so clear-cut, however, for part of the Moravain identity, the peace commitment, disappeared at the time of the Secession war. So, although the Moravian church was a peace church for several centuries, it is no longer one now. The peace commitment did not survive the interconnections between the church and the world. So, although the church is a good example of creativity, it does not fare better than its sister peace churches where our topic is concerned.

These four articles raise the following question: is separation from the world the only possible protection from the world's values? In which case the end of isolation tolls the bell of specific identity. And does it offer a lasting protection against the lures of the world? If not, separation from the world may give way to a petty and stifling atmosphere sometimes even worse than the world at large.

But the main idea behind separation from the world is (or should be) that the inner world, the spiritual world, is stronger than the outer world, and that by improving one's inner world one can influence the outer world, and be reconciled with it. One of the biblical quotations of Daniel Kauffman in his booklet is Roman 12:12: 'Be not conformed to this world, but be ye transformed by the renewing of your mind'.[4] But experience proves that too much separation from the world may hamper the renewal of the mind. This leads us to challenge McGrath in his rather manichaean view of 'harlot churches' and 'faithful churches'.

These four articles tend to show that there are times when separation from the world fosters creativity, and times when it stifles it. It is probably realistic to consider separation from the world as a temporary retreat in order to come back to the world stronger and more cheerful than ever. This happens when retreat has engendered creativity and given way to relations with the world. This problem is a permanent one with peace groups. When a group goes stale, it has not used its separation from the world in a constructive way which would inevitably have brought it back to the world, and it progressively vanishes, but when it joins the world for too long, it is also jeopardized unless it gets resourced in retreat.

A sensible attitude, maybe, is that of Friends (Quakers) who try to strike a delicate balance between faith and practice and try to live in the dialectics of separation from/reconciliation with/the world. But actually other peace groups also practice this dialectic to some extent, although they have not expressed its principle as clearly as Friends.

Only a few aspects of the questions of the relations with/or separation from/ the world for *historic peace churches* are dealt with in this small book, but we hope this will be an incentive to dig further into the topic when the opportunity arises.

NOTES
1 EAAS *Newsletter* no. 33, October 1994, p. 12.
2 William McGrath, *Separation Throughout Church History*, U.S.A., 1966, chap. V.
3 Daniel Kauffman, *1,000 Questions and Answers on points of Christian doctrine*, Scottdale, Pa, Mennonite publishing house, chap. XXVII.
4 Daniel Kauffman, *op. cit.*, p. 75.

From Witches to Spies:
Case Studies of Societal Exclusion
of New World Quakerism in the
Colonial Era

by Frédéric Limare

La femme est une menace permanente, comme si le pôle féminin
était capable, dans la représentation du monde où il est cependant
nécessaire, de détruire l'organisation symbolique qui ordonne cette
représentation.
> Sophie Houdard, *Les Sciences du Diable*, Cerf, 1992

Women are a permanent threat, as though the feminine pole was able
to destroy the symbolic organization commanding the very repre-
sentation of the world to which it is essential.

DEPICTED AS QUAINT, ERSTWHILE OR obsolete creatures, Quakers have
been presented as out of place and on the wrong time zone by their
contemporaries throughout the North American colonial era. Hence the
singling out of the Society of Friends as an historical oddity whose inad-
equacies condemn them to the byways and deadends of societal legacy.
Two case studies help us analyse the urge of society at large to segregate
Quakers as passé in a desperate effort by power-wielding groups to resist
the prophetic calling of Quaker apostasy.

The first two Quakers who set foot in New England were treated as
would-be, or to a certain extent will-be witches. These two female missionaries, Anne Austin and Mary Fisher, were forbidden to have any
contact with the New World laity. As the ship which was rumored to bring
them over to the New World was approaching the coast of New England,
the authorities of the Massachusetts Bay Colony had masterminded a
quarantine plan to quench the scourge of Quakerism. The logistics of this
high security operation were totally disproportional to the reality of the
potential threat to the New World settlement. Two middle-aged matrons

had secured a passage to the New World aboard a merchant ship. Upon landing in Boston in 1656 the two Quakeresses were swiftly spirited away to police headquarters where they were stripped down to their waists and their bodies scrutinized for stigmas alluding to witchcraft. However thorough, the search appears to have been inconclusive. Their books were burnt in an autodafé. The leaders of the colony had thereby chosen to alert public opinion to the lures and dangers of Quaker belief, allowing heathen literature to be ritualistically done away with under public eye. Having failed to establish the undeniable connection to witchcraft of the two bona fide arraigned Quakers, Puritan authorities chose to ship them back to Great Britain. A law forbidding sea captains to harbour Quakers on board was enacted. Disobedient seafarers to the New World were heavily fined, their merchandise could be shunned and backsliding trespassers were likely to endure imprisonment.

Quakerism was thus staved off rather than forcibly dealt with. By rolling back this first wavelet of contravening faith, orthodox Puritan leaders made their colony prone to witchcraze and paranoiac fears of Quaker invasion. Other zealots were bound to follow in the footsteps of these two expelled benign matrons. They could not all be sent back beyond the secure gap of the Atlantic whither they came. They would eventually be smuggled over. The point of Quakerism could not be evaded in the long run as it had been in this very first instance. Yet a precedent had been set which had bestowed on Quakerism the requisite characteristics later to endow this new and little known radical brand of Puritanism with the status of arch enemy and prime threat to the cohesion of the young colony. Highly organised and efficient in the case of these very first two Quaker immigrants to the New World, power-wielding Orthodox Puritan decision-makers had acted upon impulse though rather than unfold the first act of a rational scheme with a forethought. More often than not, this highly dramatized episode deludes us into taking too dim a view of the actual spiritual antagonism between radical Quakerism and orthodox Puritanism in mid-seventeenth century Massachusetts Bay Colony. Puritans did not hold a manichaean view of the theological bone of contention they had vis-à-vis Quakerism. Quakerism was too spiritually close a brethren to be cast beyond the pale of the Puritan church. New World Puritans were eager to steer away from what they held to be the misleading trappings of the Anglican Church. The Puritan migration had been from the beginning concerned with casting off its moorings with Anglican clerical conservatism. Furthermore, the schism was still so fresh in memories, the colony being only a couple of eventful decades old, that Puritan leaders were psychologically unable to don the garb of conservative counter-power vis-à-vis first Quakers. Even though the congregationalism of the ecclesiasts of the mid seventeenth century Bay Colony was officially non separatist, their settlement beyond the geopolitical boundaries of the Old England Anglican world view had created a de facto separation. Theirs was a split identity. They had placed an ocean between their new selves and Anglicanism, yet they vowed not to sever all ties with the Church of England so as to remain in a position later to reform and redeem it from their otherworldly plantation of God. Faced with new world Quakerism, New England Puritans endeavoured to steer a middle course between the radicalism of these dissenters and the staunch conservatism of Anglicans.[1] So, the counterbalancing influences at play in the shaping of the psyche of early New England Puritans did not allow them to take a manichaean view of radical Quaker zealots. At such an early stage in the establishment of the colony demonizing Quakers, and consequently steering themselves towards abhorred conservatism, would have jeopardized the tightrope Puritans were painstakingly walking towards the building of their new world identities. As a matter of fact, Puritan leaders shared most of the spiritual concerns their Quaker challengers upheld. They did not reject the emphasis on church purity and biblical primitivism. They shared the Quaker vindication of an intensely personalized spiritual experience.[2]

Sociologist Kai Erikson has argued that embattled Quakers and Puritans overdramatized the thin boundary separating their spiritually akin denominations. Quaker and Puritan encounters were all the harsher because enemy brothers were trying to shore up separate identities while holding fairly similar views.[3] It may be argued that Quakerism gave a radical edge to the mainstream stock market of Puritan theological tenets. Facing their deviant Quaker fellow-colonists, orthodox Puritans were in an uneasy quandary. If they chose not to curb incipient new world Quakerism, this might result in a gradual erosion of the underpinnings of Puritan theocracy for the sake of Quakerism. If, on the other hand, they opted for Quaker-baiting, they were likely to drift back to the rugged conservative end of the spectrum of their faith.

When dealing with what they referred to as the Quaker invasion which threatened to tip over the delicate balance of Puritan ruling orthodoxy from 1656 to 1660, New England leaders reenacted the very same self-defeating scenario they had rehearsed with their very first two Quaker arrivals. A trickle of zealot Quakerism ended up settling down in the new colonies. This predictable rooting of the Society of Friends kept the Bay Colony leaders at bay. Trying to expel the disease of Quakerism from the societal body of the colony was inappropriate and to no avail. From now on, Quaker conversions were sprouting from New England ground. Believers in the new faith could be numbered among the ranks of New Englanders while the official repressive policy was still bent on sending back would be dissenting immigrants.

A thoroughly researched and highly dramatized episode of the so-called Quaker invasion is the plight of prominent rebel Quakeress Mary Dyer. Actually, the crisis culminating in her 1660 hanging on Boston Common had dwindled back to nothingness after so cathartic a sacrifice. Mary, then a young woman, had walked out of the Church of Boston in the wake of defiant Ann Hutchinson during the 1636 Antinomian crisis.[4] This challenge to Puritan patriarchy by a free-spirited gifted woman could be interpreted as the first stirrings of proto-Quakerism in the new world. As a matter of fact, Mary Dyer's career provides a biographical and theological link with the Quaker invasion. In the late 1650's Mary Dyer took a business trip back to her British motherland with her enterprizing husband and sailed back to Boston a Quaker convert. Merchant William Dyer went about his business activities while his wife took upon herself to spread the word and become a missionary travelling throughout the colony. The authorities dealt with her as they had with her two predecessors. She was banished from the colony, shunned by society and pushed back beyond the outskirts of the Quaker-proof Puritan Massachusetts enclosure. Prior to her, her spiritual instigator, Ann Hutchinson had also been banished from the colony and returned to the howling wilderness where she had been killed by Indians. The violent end met by this outcast had been interpreted by Puritan orthodox leaders as a satanic gesture. In her days, Mary Dyer could find shelter in the neighbouring colony of Rhode Island. She was duly expelled to this small tolerant colony to the southern border of Massachusetts. Yet each time she surrendered to the spiritual urge of trespassing back within the limits of Massachusetts in order to face her accusers.

Labelled as a dangerous rabble-rouser, Mary Dyer brought down the fury of Puritan persecutors upon the female self. The fact that she was a woman contributed to dramatize further her clash with authorities. As with Ann Hutchinson, she was reported in contemporary accounts to be a woman of exceptional bearing and astute intellect. This outstanding person whose faith put forward that every human being was inhabited by a spark of the divine embodied a tangible threat to the Puritan hierarchy. As a matter of fact, orthodox ecclesiasts, also referred to as visible saints, believed they had been singled out to carry out the workings of God here below. Therefore, Puritan oligarchy was waging against Quaker direct democracy a bitter war on the spiritual battleground. There was no bridging the religious gap between this new female heathen contender and Governor Endicott. These Quakeresses were poles apart from their Puritan judges. This situation is reminiscent of Ann Hutchinson and John Winthrop's when the then governor of Massachusetts accused the culprit with meaning to judge her judges. With Mary Dyer, as with Ann Hutchinson, the Puritan new world order was turned upside down. They stood for the exact opposite of the theocracy they were striving to revolutionize. Wayward Quakerism was the Janus face of mainstream Puritanism. Also, Puritans were all the more determined to eradicate Quakerism from their bosom because it beckoned to unfathomable spiritual depths and potentialities lurking beneath the surface of the monolithic tip of the Puritan iceberg. Furthermore, the whole body society had metaphorically been ensconced within the aging visible saints whose retinue of deaths was interpreted as the approaching demise of the colony. With the wiping out of its first generation rulers leaving the stage at the close of long protracted careers, Massachusetts fantasized that with each buried visible saint, a candle was being snuffed out. Thus, the colony was on the verge of being benighted and reverting back to primeval chaos. Consequently, a woman in the prime of life glowing with mystical proselytizing zeal as was Mary Dyer represented the ultimate danger for Puritan orthodoxy. The near organical body metaphorization of Puritan society had caught up with orthodox theocrats who could not imagine any vista of spiritual regeneration beyond the limited scope of their natural lives. While the howling world was crashing around their ears, a preaching woman had sprung out of the spiritual wilderness spreading the word that she was enlightened with a redeeming faith. In their bewildered eyes, Mary Dyer was a harbinger of disaster whose false prophetic voice was bound to precipitate the apocalyptic collapse of the colony. The Puritan graft on America was afraid of being uprooted by radical dissent. In a desperate attempt at salvaging its jeopardized serenity, the city upon a hill had to weed out Quakerism. Significantly enough, the controversy focused on the female body of the dissenter. The tantalizer had to be kept at a safe distance and should she venture to trespass back into the colony, she was to be physically disposed of. In those days the body of Quakerism was ritualistically branded and exposed in order better to identify them as scapegoats. In fact, the 1665 *Cart and Tail Law* stipulated that dissenters found within the boundaries of the colony were to be shackled to the back of a horse cart, stripped down to the waist and whipped in every community till they reached the frontiers of Massachusetts and were then cast out.[6]

With Mary Dyer's plight, Quaker-baiting escalated to the grudging carrying out of capital punishment. On October 20, 1659 Mary Dyer was brought to the gallows along with fellow Quakers William Robinson and Marmaduke Stevenson. As she was awaiting her fate with the noose around her neck contemplating her two dead hanging companions she was theatrically saved by her own son, who galloped across Boston Common riding a white horse and brandishing a reprieve by Governor Endicott.

After this staged mock sentencing the point of Mary Dyer's execution was further belabored. Governor Endicott cringed at the prospect of holding the decision to kill that woman. In his excruciating power-wielding stalemate he could only hope his would-be victim would finally back down. Instead she further challenged the Massachusetts General Court writing angry letters for the abolition of anti-Quaker laws from her cell. She was again banished to Rhode Island from where she was not long to slip back into Massachusetts.

Mary Dyer's unflinching hankering for martyrdom finally prevailed over the misgivings of Puritan rulers. Orthodox ecclesiasts were compelled to do away with a dissenting witchlike troublemaker and in carrying out this punishment they made a symbol of freedom of religion out of her. The faith of Quakerism in the universal value of their spiritual message enabled them to volunteer from individual sacrifice thereby eroding the credibility of self-tortured Puritan executioners. In the aftermath of Mary Dyer's death, New England Puritanism could no longer claim to represent colonists in their entirety.

Separation from the mainstream theocratic ethos has thus been enforced on uncompromising Quakers This societal estrangement ushered Quakers into the realm of inner creativity and endowed them with the stamina to go through historical times as the unflinching scapegoat.

At the onset of the American Revolution, Quakerism had developed a full-fledged identity as a separate church. Their fellow colonists set up numerous hurdles to keep them away from the march of history. Yet, in the face of adversity, Quakerism abided by the role of upholder of universal moral conscience they had inherited from their hardships in the early colonial period. Insuperable obstacles such as the plight of a pacifist church in the midst of military turmoil gave way to creative role playing into the war such as relief work. This is why the paradox of interlocked participation and separation vis-à-vis mainstream history in the colonial time deserves to be underlined.

NOTES
1 William K.B. Stoever, *A Faire and Easy Way to Heaven: Covenant Theology and Antinomianism in Early Massachusetts*, Middletown, Connecticuit, Wesleyan University Press, 1978.
2 Carla Gardina Pestana: *Quakers and Baptists in Colonial Massachusetts*, Cambridge University Press, 1991.
3 Kai Erikson, *Wayward Puritans*, New York, John Wiley, 1960.
4 *Ibid.*
5 *Ibid.*
6 Ruth Plimpton, *Mary Dyer, Biography of a Rebel Quaker*, Boston, Branden Publishing Company, 1994.

Separation from the World as a Source of Creativity, then of Sterility, for Nantucket Quakers in the 18th and 19th Centuries

by Professor Jeanne Henriette Louis

Nantucket Quakers in American literature: from St John de Crèvecoeur to Robert Lowell

NANTUCKET QUAKERS BECAME FAMOUS in the United States and in France mainly through Saint John de Crèvecoeur's *Letters from an American Farmer* (1782 and 1784) written after the writer's visit to the island in 1777. The Letters on Nantucket (IV-VIII) take more than one third of the English version of the book. Crèvecoeur's *Letters* are a mixture of mythology and reality which show Nantucket as a paradise, the more easily separated from the world as it is an island. One misleading assertion in the *Letters* on Nantucket spread the idea that the first European settlers on Nantucket were Friends, which is wrong. The author writes: 'thus have enthusiasm and persecution both in Europe as well as here, been the cause of the most arduous undertakings.... The peculiar genius of their sect inspired them with the same spirit of moderation which was exhibited at Pennsylvania'.[1]

In his poem 'The Exiles' published in 1843, John Greenleaf Whittier refers to Thomas Macy's flight to Nantucket.[2] The first settlers appear as heroes, victims of Puritan persecution, and apostles of liberty. They were, indeed, men (and their families) who felt uncomfortable with Puritans' excessive authority. Many of these first settlers' descendants were going to become Friends in the eighteenth century. So although these settlers were not Friends, they shaped the background from which Quakerism sprang on Nantucket a few decades later, and Whittier celebrated them. With Melville's *Moby Dick*, published in 1851, the image of contemporary Nantucket Quakers had been considerably tarnished. Melville describes Quaker Captain Bildad as someone particularly rough with his crew.

Then in his poem 'The Quaker graveyard of Nantucket' dedicated to his cousin Warren Winslow, a 19th century Nantucket Quaker dead at sea, Robert Lowell gives a definitely negative image of Nantucket Quakers. He writes: 'The wind's wings beat upon the stones, Cousin, and scream for you and the claws rush at the sea's throat of this old Quaker graveyard where the bones cry out in the long night for the hurt beast...'. And he gives the following precision: 'All you recovered from Poseidon died with you, my cousin, and the harrowed brine is fruitless'.[3] The very concept of sterility is brought by this last verse.

From Crèvecoeur's enthusiasm to Lowell's dejection, the image of Nantucket Quakers has been so tarnished that we may wonder where Nantucket Quaker creativity has gone, what was the impact of separation from the world on this once predominant religious group on the island? Relying on history as much as possible, this essay will try to answer the following questions: how did Quakerism actually grow in Nantucket, what relations did it nurture towards the world, and what were the limits of its creativity?

The insular dream of the first purchasers

In spite of Crèvecoeur's assertions that the first settlers were Friends, we must keep in mind that Quakerism was only officially born on the island in 1708, half a century after the beginning of the European settlement. The island had been bought in 1641 together with Martha's Vineyard and the Elizabethan islands by Thomas Mayhew from Lord Sterling and Sir Ferdinando Georges who had royal grants on it. Thomas Mayhew was a Puritan priest who was closer to Roger Williams than to other Puritan priests. Whereas Mayhew settled down on Martha's Vineyard, no European settlement took place on Nantucket before 1659, after Thomas Mayhew had sold the island to ten British purchasers.

The first one interested in the purchase was Thomas Macy, who happened to have given shelter to three Quakers fleeing Puritan persecution. Macy was no Friend, he was a Baptist. He was only a Quaker sympathizer in that he sided with the victims against the persecutors, but by giving these Quakers shelter, he had disobeyed the law and was given a thirty pounds fine. And it happened that two of the Quakers he had sheltered, William Robinson and Marmaduke Stephenson, were hanged by the Puritans in Boston in December 1659. When Macy heard about Nantucket being for sale, he saw there a good opportunity to get a little farther away from the continent. Insular life, separated from the main land, appealed to those who suffered from the stifling atmosphere of Massachusetts. The other purchasers, Edward Starbuck, William Pike, Tristam Coffin, Peter Coffin, Richard Swayne, Thomas Bernard, Christopher Hussey, Stephen Greenleaf, were also influenced by the Baptist and Anabaptist movements, and were glad to get away from Puritan authority.[4]

It happened that one of the first buyers, John Swain, had become a member of the Religious Society of Friends after he settled on Nantucket. Then in 1667, a second Quaker settled down on the island. She was Sarah Shattuck Gardner. In 1672, a third Quaker came to the island: Stephen Hussey, but it seems that none of these Quakers was very influential.[5] Although the magistrates on the island were supposed to be liberal, they were opposed to Quaker presence on the island.

Quaker beginnings on Nantucket

From 1680, two Quaker colonies grew on Cape Cod – in Falmouth and Yarmouth, which made the threat of Quaker invasion closer than ever. Visits of Quaker 'missionaries' were forbidden until 1696. The ban was lifted during this year, so that the British Quaker missionaries who visited the continent started including Nantucket in their route.

Thomas Chalkley first came in 1698, and he found the audience was receptive. He particularly noticed Mary Coffin Starbuck as a potential spiritual leader. He was planning to come back in 1704. John Richardson was the second visitor in 1701. This visit confirmed Mary Coffin Starbuck in her attraction for Quakerism. John Richardson encouraged her to found a Quaker group on the island.[6]

Thomas Story, one of William Penn's close collaborators in Pennsylvania, came to the island in 1704, and convinced Mary to start a Quaker group on the island, which she did shortly after his visit. Between 1704 and 1708, Nantucket was visited by Richard Harper, Mary Slocum and John Butler. In 1705, Samuel Bownas preached there. In 1706, Mary Banister and Ann Chapman from England, Hugh Copperwait from Long Island, Peleg Slocum from Dartmouth, and William Anthony from Rhode Island also preached there. Then a few others as well. In 1708 a letter was addressed to the Yearly Meeting in Rhode Island asking for permission to set up a Yearly Meeting on the island. Permission was given, and the Quaker group of Nantucket was officially born. Mary Starbuck became the Elder and her son Nathaniel was secretary. During the following years the group grew permanently, and several Meeting Houses were built. In the late 1750's, the Meeting House on Pleasant and Main housed 1,500 people. In 1762, the Quaker community having still grown to 2,400 people, the main Meeting House was again enlarged.[7]

Isolation from the continent as a source of creative relations with the Algonquins, Nantucket's native Americans

The comparatively good relations between white settlers and the Algonquins on Nantucket in the second half of the 17th century do not yet correspond to a period when settlers were Quakers, but they witness the originality of the human background from which Quakerism sprang shortly afterwards.

Thomas Mayhew, the first purchaser of Martha's Vineyard and Nantucket, had been inspired by Roger William's dealing with the natives in Rhode Island. He initiated good relations with the natives on the two islands by calling a conference with the Algonquins in 1644, and telling them that the white settlers on these islands would buy their lands at a fair price and that they meant to live in peace with them. And those who bought Nantucket from Mayhew in 1659 kept his promise.

The key figure in the good relations with the natives was Peter Folger, who later became Benjamin Franklin's grandfather through his daughter Abiah. Peter Folger was a school teacher, blacksmith and surveyor on Martha's Vineyard. He helped Mayhew settle on the island, and he learnt the Algonquins' language. He first acted as translator between Mayhew and the natives, and from 1659 he helped Edward Starbuck settle on Nantucket, surveying the land bought from the Algonquins, and making sure that the latter agreed with the transactions. The Algonquins trusted him very much. Peter Folger had become a Baptist in 1659, and he moved with his family to Rhode Island in 1662. But they did not stay there long: in the summer of 1663 the first purchasers of Nantucket invited Peter Folger to settle down on Nantucket with his family as a half-shareman provided he would play the role of interpreter between them and the Algonquins. Folger accepted.[8]

As soon as 1665, Nantucket had an opportunity to show that its values in human relationships were a little different from what usually took place on the continent. The first native converted to Christianity by Peter Folger was Assamoogh, a very intelligent young man. When he became a Christian, Peter Folger gave him an English name: John Gibbs. The first settlers on Nantucket sent John Gibbs to Harvard University to study for the ministry, after which he came back to Nantucket to act as minister to his own people.[9] But John Gibbs had an enemy among native Americans on the continent: Metacomet, one of the sons of Massasoit, who had welcomed the Pilgrims at Plymouth in 1621. Metacomet had been sent to England to be educated. His English name was Philip. Philip succeeded his father as grand sachem of the Wampanoag Confederation, and was called King Philip by the white men. He meant eventually to lead a native rebellion against the Whites in New England.

But in 1665 Philip said he had to take John Gibbs' life because the latter had insulted the memory of his dead father. He landed on Nantucket with a large fleet of war canoes and told the local chief, Attychat, that he wanted John Gibbs to be surrendered to him. The natives on the island were appalled. They helped Gibbs to hide in a swamp and quickly called

Peter Folger for help. Without any weapon, Peter Folger faced Philip, and succeeded in talking him out of the island. From this time the Nantucket Algonquins' loyalty to Peter Folger became absolute, and also benefited the other Whites on the island.[10]

When King Philip's war broke out on the continent in 1675, Philip tried to draw Nantucket Algonquins into the war on his side. But the latter knew better. Because they had been treated in a comparatively fair way, they remained neutral, and just kept away from the war on the continent. Nantucket remained a peaceful island throughout the war. It was separated from the turmoils of the continent, and even became a refuge for Nantucket settlers' relatives and friends who fled violence in Massachusetts and even Rhode Island.

So, in this case, geographical separation went along with creative attitudes in the relations between Whites and natives. Peter Folger had played a key role in this. He never became a Quaker, but as a Baptist, he was sympathetic to Quakers and was the spiritual father of Mary Coffin Starbuck, who started the first Quaker Meeting on Nantucket. Peter Folger also wrote the poem 'A Looking-Glass for our Time' which took the defense of Quakers and Anabaptists accused by Puritans of being responsible for King Philip's War on the continent.

The growth of a Quaker culture

A Quaker culture was progressively born in Nantucket. Although Saint John de Crèvecoeur certainly exaggerated and idealized this Quaker culture, Nantucket had become a more creative place than the average colonial town. Simplicity was and still is a feature of Nantucket architecture. When John Woolman came in 1760 he was happy to notice the simplicity of life in Nantucket which was a contrast to the ostentation of Philadelphia Quakers. He himself spoke to the women Quakers, as he records in his Journal: 'reminding them that the more plain and simple their way of living was, the less need of running great hazards to support them in it. Showing, as the way opened, that, where people were truly humble, used themselves to business, and were content with a plain way of life, it had ever been attended with more true peace and calmness of mind than they have had who, aspiring to greatness and outward show, have grasped hard for an income to support themselves in it'.[11] Nantucket Quakers were considered by Philadelphia Quaker reformists like John Woolman as a haven for Quaker principles whereas Philadelphia Quakerism had partly gone astray. Family life was a prime value. Experience and example were more valued than authority and academic teaching. Children grew in a very affectionate atmosphere and women were given spiritual responsibilities.

Quakerism, whaling and creativity

But then, of course, creativity expressed itself in the development of the whaling fisheries. The family that most embodies the combination of Quakerism, whaling and creativity seems to be the Rotch family.

Joseph Rotch was born in Salem, Massachusetts in 1704. He was trained as a cordwainer and migrated to Nantucket in 1725. He entered the Macy family by marrying Love Macy in 1733 and in the same year he joined the Quaker group of Nantucket. This opened up for him access to the whaling industry. He thus became part of the Nantucket mainstream. In 1753 he was at the head of the Macy firm. He then started trading directly with merchants in Connecticut, Rhode Island, New York and even London, bypassing the middlemen. In 1764 he split his firm into two separate companies and at the end of 1765 he went to Dartmouth on the continent in search of a suitable location to start a whaling business. He settled there with his son Joseph Jr. in 1767. He called the place he bought Bedford village, a name that was later changed to New Bedford. With the opening of shipyards, blacksmith shops, rope walks, cooperages, and other industries necessary to the whale-fisheries, New Bedford was now able to outfit its own ships instead of relying on Nantucket. The first candle manufactory was established in 1768 under the guidance of Joseph Rotch. By 1771 both sides of the river were bustling with activity. Joseph Rotch died in 1784, but his son William moved there from Nantucket in 1795, and with his two younger brothers Francis and Joseph, carried on the family business.[12] So, here is a case where the island influenced the continent.

The eldest son, William Rotch was apprenticed to his father from a young age. In 1772 he conceived the making of candles in Nantucket. From this time the Rotch firms built their own ships, set them whaling round the world, made candles, sold their candles and oil. In 1754 William Rotch married Elizabeth Barney, born in a Quaker family. William was much more committed to Quakerism than his father. He became creative both in the religious Society of Friends and in the whaling business. He and his family settled down in Dunkerque, France, with other Nantucket Quakers from 1786. William Rotch and his wife came back to Nantucket in 1793 because they found that the French revolution was worse than the American one in terms of violence. In the following year they moved to New Bedford, where they spent the rest of their lives.

Neutrality as separation from the world

A culture of neutrality also developed on the island during the 18th century. Although Nantucket was often the victim of aggressions by French pirate boats, the Quaker culture tended to discourage self-defense.

Both the island and its ships suffered great losses from the French during Queen Anne's war (1701-1713) and King George's war (1744-1748). From 1760 the French were no longer to be feared on the seas.

At the time of the American revolution, Nantucketers found that neutrality was the only bearable position. They were attracted to it by their geographical position, by whaling and by Quakerism. In February 1775 the Restraining Act was introduced in Parliament, forbidding the New England colonies to trade with any nation but Britain and the British West Indies and, most important to the islanders, barred New Englanders from the north Atlantic fisheries. Edmund Burke and David Barclay supported Nantucket's cause, and as a result the island was exempted from this Act.[13] In spite of the 'privilege', all in all the island suffered from both sides during the Independence war, but at least it embodied an alternative to war and violence. Neutrality did not so much prove separation from the world as it revealed connection to two worlds which fought each other: the revolted colonies and Britain. Neutrality meant a lack of identification to any of the warring parties, but it also meant capability to communicate with both. At its best, Nantucket's neutrality was in the line of Pennsylvania's creativity at the time of the Holy Experiment. So, here again, acting differently from the colonies at large meant creativity.

The leading figure who rooted Nantucket in its position of neutrality was William Rotch, himself at the junction of whaling and Quaker creativity. He saw Nantucket's attitude as an extension of William Penn's Holy Experiment which ended up in 1756, and so did the reformist Quakers of Pennsylvania. And this experiment in neutrality enabled William Rotch to speak in favor of a non-violent revolution when at the Assemblée Nationale in France in 1791 together with French Quaker Jean de Marcillac, while he and other Nantucketers were spending a few years in Dunkerque.

Creativity in the resolution of conflicts

One aspect of Nantucket's creativity and Quaker culture was the fact that lawyers were practically absent from it for decades, as Crèvecoeur related in his *Letters from an American Farmer* and as Robert Mooney and André Sigourney explain in *The Nantucket way*. The two authors are lawyers and they were struck by the fact that not one professional lawyer lived on the island in the colonial era. In the Quaker culture, the professional lawyer is no more necessary than the professional Minister. Direct conflict resolution or resolution through non-professional mediation were very much part of Nantucket Quaker culture in the colonial era. There were strifes, tensions, but they seldom degenerated into physical violence. Besides, crime was mostly absent from Nantucket at this time because society on this small island was closely knit. Policemen and Justices were idle. Physical separation from the mainland connected with the Quaker culture gave Nantucket a reputation of purity in the 18th century, which accounts for Crèvecoeur's admiration.

The seminal role of Nantucket in the abolitionist movement

Nantucket Quakerism also played a creative role towards the abolition of African Americans' slavery. In November 1716 it was recorded in the Minutes of the Nantucket Meeting as 'not agreeable for Friends to purchase slaves and keep them Term of life'. In April 1717 the record says: 'Our aged friend John Farmer presented this meeting with an epistle concerning Negroes which was read'.[14] In 1730, the Quaker author Elihu Coleman wrote a famous tract 'against the despicable practice of making slaves of men', which served as a direct forerunner of the Abolitionist movement which flourished in New England.[15] In 1760, when he visited Nantucket, John Woolman wrote: 'I had to encourage them to be content without slaves; making mention of the numerous troubles and Vexations which frequently attend the Minds of People who depend on Slaves to do their Labour'.[16] In 1770, William Rotch declared the freedom of Absalom Boston, a black mariner who had served on Rotch ships and demonstrated unusual nautical ability. Boston's former master came to Nantucket and attempted to regain possession of Boston as his personal property, but a Nantucket judge and jury declared him a free man. The owner, disgusted with Island justice, threatened to carry his case to an appeals court in Boston, but William Rotch retained the counsel of John Adams to handle the defense, and the matter went no further.[17] Nantucket followed the example of William Rotch, and thereafter its Quakers never kept slaves. Absalom Boston became America's first black whaling captain, recruited an all-black crew, and sailed away into the Pacific as master of his own ship.

Mooney and Sigourney also relate that in 1822 a fugitive slave named Arthur Cooper who had settled on Nantucket was confronted by his owner on his very doorstep, but was rescued by an aroused mob and sheltered by the Quakers until his pursuers fled the island.[18] So, Quaker Nantucket played the role of a haven for this fugitive, as Quaker New Bedford did at the same period. But Nantucket being an island, the haven was more efficient, and, in any case, the Quaker culture of New Bedford originated in Nantucket. Quakerism was the largest religious denomination in New Bedford at the beginning of the 19th century, and between 1809 and 1850, the black population of New Bedford grew to almost 700.

William Lloyd Garrison was aware of Nantucket's support of the abolitionist movement, and he often visited the island on his lecture-tours and fund-raising drives.

Nantucket even completed the role of New Bedford in the liberation and promotion of Frederick Douglass. A fugitive from Maryland, Frederick Douglass had spent his first three years as a free man in New Bedford, where he had been helped by Quakers. On the evening of August 16th, 1841, the anti-slavery society organized a meeting based on a lecture by William Lloyd Garrison. Seated in the audience was a group of off-island visitors from New Bedford. Among them was Frederick Douglass. The young African American was asked to improvise a personal contribution about his experience as a slave. At first he was very shy, and impressed by the silence of the Quaker audience. But because he felt their sympathy, he spoke beautifully, and delivered the first and greatest speech of his life. When the meeting broke up, Frederick Douglass was immediately invited by John Collins to become a public speaker for the Anti-slavery society.[19] Thus was Frederick Douglass's destiny as a free man shaped both by New Bedford and Nantucket where the Quaker influence was still dominant.

In any case Nantucket was destined to become a leader in the field of human rights since Lucretia Coffin Mott was born in 1793 on Fair Street on the island.

Climax and decline of the Nantucket meeting

But although Nantucket Quakerism could still play this role in 1841, it was already declining. Throughout the 18th century, the steady increase in the number of members had been a sign of good health and vigor for the Society of Friends on the island. The number of Members had grown from 222 in 1733 to 310 in 1738 and 409 in 1743 to reach 2,400 in 1763, as already mentioned, and Alexander Starbuck writes that the records of the Society contain several interesting entries showing the spirit of friendliness among the members of the sect at this time. In 1793 the new Meeting-House was ready for occupancy and the removal took place immediately after.[20] With the building of the new Meeting-House came a separation into two congregations. William Rotch became clerk of the North Meeting.

Separation into two Meeting-Houses in the 18th century only meant success and growth. The relations between the Meeting-Houses were good. Thus, during the last decade of the 18th century and the first decade of the 19th century the Nantucket Friends reached the summit of their strength. They emerged from the period of the revolution still vigorous. Henry Barnard Worth writes: 'When the nineteenth century opened, there were two Quaker Meetings largely attended and flourishing, and the only other sect on the island was still struggling and weak'.[21]

But in 1829 the two Meeting-Houses were no longer needed, which was a bad sign for the Quaker group on the island. Besides Nantucket was not immune from the division among Friends on the continent. The rupture took place in 1827-1828. The followers of Elias Hicks were known as the 'Liberal Branch' while those who clung to the old organization were known as 'Orthodox Friends'.

Elias Hicks had been dead several months when the doctrines he enunciated gained a firm foothold in Nantucket. In the summer of 1830 a follower of Hicks visited the island and appointed a time for a Meeting to be held. The Friends who attended the Meeting were disowned. Then another cleavage took place. A Gurney faction was formed. Orthodox Friends disapproved of Gurney because he prepared what he would say at Meetings.

Less than a decade elapsed before there was another secession from the ranks, this time especially affecting the Gurney faction. A reversion struggle began in 1838 under the leadership of John Wilbur, from Rhode Island. And the Supreme Court sustained the Gurneyites and declared that the Wilburites had seceded from the parent body. The Nantucket Friends who continued their allegiance to the New England Yearly Meeting as Gurneyites met at the house of Cromwell Barnard, calling themselves the Nantucket Monthly Meeting of Friends. Peleg Mitchell having been identified with the Wilburites was adjudged by the dissenters as not suitable as Clerk, and in his stead was chosen William Mitchell.

The Wilburites built a new house of worship and occupied it in 1850. They were disowned by the Gurneyites. The Gurneyites imposed a law suit on the Wilburites for the possession of Fair Street Meeting. In 1864 the Meeting-House and land on Fair Street were sold and the proceeds as well as the cash were divided by agreement between the two meetings. Nantucket Quakerism had been hit by sterile strife and did not recover from this in the 19th century. In 1894 only one member of the Meeting lived at Nantucket, and it was decided to sell the Meeting-House. It was therefore sold in June 1894.[22]

The divisions between Hicksites, Gurneyites and Wilburites are paradoxical. Hicks was reproached by his opponents for relying too much on divine guidance, not enough on the Bible, whereas Gurneyites were reproached by their opponents for relying too much on the Bible, and not letting the spirit guide them. Wilburites called themselves the only orthodox Friends, against all changes, relying on the Inner Light. But the attraction of such leaders as Hicks and Gurney came from the fact that Orthodox Friends had failed to keep the spirit moving. Their separation from the world was no longer connected with creativity, but with sterility and dryness. They enforced their discipline with a narrow mind and lost the sense of Quaker identity whereas they claimed they were preserving it. Throughout the 19th century they self-destroyed their group through disownment of members for what looked vital to them, and now looks trivial to many contemporary Friends. The main causes for disownment were: getting married outside the Society of Friends; not dressing plainly enough; attending a wedding performed by a minister; drinking alcohol; attending meetings at the Methodist Society; owning a musical instrument in one's house; singing and dancing. Thus the Quaker group in many cases lost its creative members and kept the tedious ones.

Paradoxically the Gurneyites were more open to the outside world: they allowed marriage with non-members, attending meetings of other societies, and did not discipline dressing. But because they were more fundamentalist in their inspiration than the other groups, they were not the best representatives of the Quaker identity either.

This could explain why Quakerism died out on Nantucket at the end of the 19th century. Separation from the world had become compulsory for the wrong reasons. A series of petty rules turned Quakerism on the island into a moralizing stifling group, not so very different from the Puritan world from which the first settlers had tried to escape. The logical result was the self-destruction of a 'house divided against itself'.

The combination of whaling and Quakerism, which hit Nantucket Quakerism, also hit New Bedford Quakerism in the long run. In New Bedford, as in Nantucket, whaling and Quakerism both collapsed, but it all happened later.

Of course, when Quakerism had practically died out on the island, it no longer influenced the world, although the plain architecture of Nantucket is still preserved and valued nowadays.

Conclusion: Separation from the world as a sign of pioneering or autism?

Separation from the world usually means defiance towards the world, combined with a need for protection from the world in order to preserve cherished values. The first European British settlers on Nantucket took refuge there away from Puritan intolerance. Many of their descendants became Friends. They became rich through whaling, and traded with the world. They became creative in Quakerism and whaling at the same time. They influenced the world, particularly as regards the abolition of slavery. They were pioneers in the 18th century and the beginning of the 19th century. But Quakerism did not survive the downfall of whaling, and became insular and provincial. It was influenced by the strife of continental Quakerism and its geographical insular position became a weakness: Quakerism was torn by these strifes and became sterile. The spirit had died out, the creativity had been stifled, and had gone. This explains the change from Crèvecoeur's *Letters to an American Farmer* to Robert Lowell's 'the Quaker graveyard on Nantucket'. Maybe making money out of the killing of whales had killed the spirit of Quakerism in the long run. Quaker creativity had grown together with whaling creativity, but both collapsed together. The problem of relations with the world became critical on Nantucket as it had been in Pennsylvania when it brought the downfall of the Holy Experiment.

NOTES

1 Saint John de Crèvecoeur, *Letters from an American Farmer*, New York, Dutton, 1957, p. 98.
2 John Greenleaf Whittier, *Lays of my Home*, Boston, William Ticknor, 1843.
3 Robert Lowell, *Lord Weary's Castle*, 1944, p. 7.
4 Alexander Starbuck, *The History of Nantucket: county, island, and town*, Rutland, Verlont, Charles Tuttle cy, 1969.
5 Robert Leach, 'Why Nantucket Quakers?' II, 13-14.
6 cf. Frédéric Limare, *The Quaker New World's Journal, 1689-1736*. Mémoire de Maîtrise, Université de Paris VII, 1984.
7 Alexander Starbuck, *op. cit.*, pp. 525-530.
8 King Clarence, *The half-share man. Peter Folger of Nantucket, Grandfather of Benjamin Franklin*, Nantucket Historical Trust, 1972, chap. XIII.
9 Mooney Robert & Sigourney André, *The Nantucket Way*, New York, Doubleday, p. 15.
10 *Ibid.*, p. 19.
11 John Woolman, *The Journal and Major Essays*, Ed. by Phillip P. Moulton, Friends United Press, Richmond, Indiana, 1989.
12 Judith Boss and Joseph Thomas, *New Bedford, a Pictorial History*, Virginia Beach, The Donning Cy Publishers, 1983, p. 26.
13 Edward Byers, *The Nation of Nantucket*, Boston, Northwestern University Press, 1987, p. 203.
14 Alexander Starbuck, *op. cit.*, p. 533.
15 cf. Jean R. Soderlund, *Quakers and Slavery*, Princeton University Press, 1985, p. 23, note 18.
16 *Journal of John Woolman, op. cit.*, p. 115.
17 Mooney & Sigourney, *op. cit.*, p. 140.
18 *Ibid.*
19 *Ibid.*
20 Alexander Starbuck, *op. cit.*, p. 536.
21 Henry Barnard Worth, 'Quakerism on Nantucket since 1800', *Nantucket Historical Association*, vol. I, Bulletin no. I, p. 7.
22 *Ibid.*, passim.

Uneasy Citizens: An Essay on the Difficulties of Creating a Mennonite Politics

by Frederic Fransen, Ph.D

Part I – Anabaptist 'anti-politics'

THE WORD 'POLITICS' IS DERIVED from the ancient Greek word 'politika' meaning 'things of the city'. From almost the beginning of monotheistic religion, in the story of the Tower of Babel (Genesis XI: 1-9), we learn of the extreme difficulty of uniting city life – that is political life – with a life of faith. It is not surprising, therefore, that a community of believers such as the Mennonites would show an aversion to politics.

This essay will address the successes and failures of Mennonites in their efforts to create a new understanding of politics. Although there have been a number of attempts at examining Mennonite political views, they have almost exclusively done so from a theological or sociological/historical perspective.[1] I intend, in contrast, to look at Mennonite politics from the perspective of politics. In this way, I hope to provide some probing questions which might raise further interest and discussion in this area.

The Anabaptist movement, of which Mennonites form a part, originated almost at the beginning of the Reformation, with the first adult baptism taking place in 1525 in Zurich.[2] This form of 'believer's baptism' was immediately considered subversive to the city, and the first Anabaptist execution took place in 1527, also in Zurich. Why were the Anabaptists considered so dangerous? On the one hand, throughout the period of religious persecution, all those, Catholics and non-Catholics, who persecuted dissenters thought they were doing what was in the best interests of their subjects. Not to be baptized meant for them a certain trip to hell when one left this world. Through not baptizing their children, the Anabaptists were condemning innocent souls, and the church, whose role it was to protect their flocks against eternal damnation, refused to stand by and let it happen. Among adults, disrespect for the authority of the church was also a bad influence in the city and needed, therefore, to be put down with all necessary force.

Apart from the effect which Anabaptist beliefs had on Anabaptists' souls and the souls of their children, strictly from the point of view of the rulers of the city, Anabaptists were even more nefarious. To understand why, it is necessary to begin with the philosophy behind what makes a city good. For Plato, for instance, in addition to the proper size and a fertile and defensible location, a city must be in harmony with itself (*The Republic*, 432a). To be in harmony with itself, of course, does not mean that all differences among citizens must be wiped out, but rather that the ruler must weave together the different elements of his community into a single whole (*The Statesman*, 307d-309b).

The means by which a ruler accomplishes this are varied, but there are a couple of common threads. First, in one way or another, it is necessary to achieve a sense of common origin[3] and second, it is necessary to ensure that at certain important moments and in certain especially vital areas, such as birth, maturity, marriage and death, each citizen is made aware of his dependence on and obligation to the city. Here is where the Anabaptists' refusal to baptize their children became subversive.

By denying the ritual of automatic baptism, Anabaptists no longer were willing to participate in the harmony of the city. Their separation created the possibility, indeed the necessity, that the city would no longer be united. For the Anabaptists, the city was no longer the place where goodness was to be strived for, because there was a threshold of goodness necessary for entry into God's kingdom. The kind of homogenizing of different people, despite their level of faith, which the state church practiced was not desirable. The effect of this was to destroy the possibility of creating a good city by destroying the possibility of creating a whole city. The difficulty which Mennonites encounter today when trying to create a viable understanding of politics is that they constantly run back into the original question of this separation of God's Kingdom (which they assume they are a part of and understand better than other Christians and non-Christians) from the Kingdom of Man which the city represents.

For the most part, Mennonites, throughout their history have avoided interaction with government as much as possible, limiting their contacts to corporate negotiations over settlements, their status as conscientious objectors, and business (primarily agricultural) contracts.[4] In the United States, Swiss Mennonites in the Eastern states eschewed public offices, voting and serving in the armed forces.[5] In Prussia and Russia, Mennonites sometimes served as mayors of all-Mennonite villages and in representations to the Russian government, but until 1870, based on their agreement with Catherine the Great, they held special privileges including exemption from military service.[6] The withdrawal of the military exemption and later the general deterioration of living conditions brought on by the Bolsheviks led to a series of migrations to North America.

Once either group had settled in North America, however, content on their farms and in their communities, they lived a happily apolitical life until World War I.[7] During World War I, as German-speakers who also refused to fight or to buy war bonds, Mennonites were ridiculed, attacked, jailed, and humiliated. Their houses were splattered with yellow paint, and several mock-lynchings occurred. The war came to an end rather quickly, however, before much collective action was taken.

The traditional response of Mennonites to an intolerable political environment had always been emigration. When the famine began in Russia in the 1920's, however, the immediate needs of Russian Mennonites led them to appeal to their cousins (from earlier migrations) for help. The aid which was organized involved not only Russian Mennonites in North America, but also Swiss Mennonites, and led to the first pan-Mennonite organization, Mennonite Central Committee (MCC), formed in 1920.[8]

After the famine relief program ended, MCC faded, but was again revived as World War II began. In order to avoid the troubles of World War I, Mennonites, along with Brethren and Quakers, lobbied for legislation recognizing conscientious objectors. The result was a program called Civilian Public Service in which Mennonites, along with other objectors, built and administered camps in which draftees were allowed to do alternative service.[9]

Mennonite Central Committee continued to provide possibilities for alternative service during the Korean and Vietnam wars. Following the Vietnam War and the end of the draft in the United States, it has continued to exist as a relief, development, and peace organization. In this third context, it has sponsored and supported a number of different organizations and activities, from the victim-offender reconciliation program, Christian Peacemaker Teams, Mennonite Reconciliation Services, and NATO Watch. Each of these efforts, beginning with Mennonite Central Committee itself, has been an effort in one way or another to involve Mennonites in the world, and particularly in the world of politics. This involvement, of whatever kind, has led to an important change in Mennonite attitudes toward the state, which finds its turning point in World War II. Let me make explicit the importance of the change in the Mennonite world view which I believe the Mennonite response to this war provoked.

The Anabaptist denial of the concept of the state-church left them with two possible directions in their relations to the state. They could either re-form (or take over) a new state, and establish a theocracy. Or they could deny the reality of the state altogether and withdraw from it. At various times, Anabaptists have tried both of these solutions. During the initial flowering of the movement in Germany, they took over the city of Münster, and proclaimed the Kingdom of God. A short time later, the city was recaptured, the Anabaptists converted, and the leaders hung from the cathedral (their cages still hang from the steeple there). Anabaptists were also the leaders of an armed revolt at Waldshut, in Southern Germany.[10]

The other possible consequence of their understanding of the state, withdrawing from the world, turned out to have more staying power than the Münsterite uprising. Whereas the Anabaptist movement was primarily a movement of the cities in the early sixteenth century, by the end of that century it had become rural and agrarian. Living in small, isolated villages, Mennonites were able to govern themselves. Dissent was met by excommunication (or also shunning in the case of the Amish), which is only possible in a context which is at once homogeneous and surrounded by an external society. According to the Schleitheim Confession, the first and perhaps most important Anabaptist statement of Faith, Anabaptists are to leave the world: 'Truly all creatures are in but two classes, good and bad, believing and unbelieving, darkness and light, the world and those who have come out of the world ...'[11] For centuries afterwards, separation from the world was to drive the understanding of Anabaptists in their relation to politics.

Had the relation between church and state remained as straightforward as it was in the sixteenth century, this thesis would have been easier to analyze. Submission to state-church baptisms and other sacraments would be an easy test to apply. However, as other denominations have adopted the practice of adult baptism, and as a state church is forbidden in the United States and hardly exists in Canada, the problem becomes more difficult. The test of Mennonite acknowledgement of the state must be sought in other areas.

At about the same time as the state became less concerned about religion, the other main exceptionalist characteristic of Mennonites began to become important: Mennonite pacifism. In this area it is still possible to analyze the way Mennonites view politics, and to judge the consequences of their views.

Anabaptist pacifism has basically the same origin as adult baptism. The early Mennonites believed that the Kingdom of God was about to be realized, and that it was essential to live out a true Christian life according to the Bible in order to participate in it. As all the baptisms in the Bible were of confessing adults, it was essential also to baptize only confessing adults. And, as non-resistance to violence was practiced by

Jesus, self-defense was not considered legitimate for Mennonites.[12] Given the principle of non-resistance and given that Mennonites were hunted by the state's army, participation in the military was not considered by the early Mennonites. For them there was no question of developing the kind of nuanced positions on just wars such as other denominations held. The state was literally their enemy, and the question of allying with that enemy against some external foe was incomprehensible.

For the Mennonites living in the United States, the advantages of religious tolerance included being left relatively alone during early American wars, and being allowed to hire replacements when the Civil War instituted the draft. Mennonites in northern Europe assured themselves an easy solution to the problem by getting a corporate exemption to military service in Prussia and Russia, and emigrating each time that exemption was revoked. The challenge to the principle of non-resistance through compulsory military service, therefore, really only arose for North American Mennonites in World War I and in the wars which followed it.[13]

The issue of the draft has been complicated and difficult for Mennonites to address. Traditionally, when Mennonites are faced by a problem, they resort first to the New Testament in their search for an answer. When the Zurich militia came to try to force them to recant their beliefs about baptism, the parallel to Jesus' non-resistance was easy to find, and if carrying out that aspect of discipleship meant death, at least it was unambiguous.

The problem is no more difficult theologically, and much less costly personally, when the army comes to ask one to join. For Mennonites living after the religious wars but before the draft, it was easy enough simply to say 'no'. As subjects – but not citizens – Mennonites felt no obligation to serve the country in which they lived, precisely because it wasn't 'their' country.[14]

With the advent of the draft, however, avoiding the problem was no longer possible. What the draft did was to bring to the surface again the original problem which Mennonites faced concerning membership in the city. Participation in the draft was made a condition of good citizenship, and good citizenship made a requirement for living in the state. In effect, this re-posed the original problem of membership in the state. What the draft meant was that Mennonites were no longer allowed to mind their own business. Instead, as the price of religious tolerance, they were asked to acknowledge the existence of the state, or, in other words, to prove their loyalty and good citizenship.

In the period surrounding World War II, this took several forms. In many churches German was abandoned as the language of worship, a process which had begun during World War I. Many American churches also, for the first time and following an older American tradition, began placing flags in the sanctuary.[15] They did this to acknowledge their gratitude to a state which had offered tolerance and opportunity, and to display their loyalty in a country where flags carry great symbolism. Finally, MCC lobbied for a recognized form of alternate service in which Mennonites could participate in the draft without having to join the army.[16]

The de facto acknowledgment of their citizenship and of the state which these gestures of patriotism indicate marks a watershed in Mennonite relations to the state. It also marks the end, in philosophical terms – and the beginning of the end, in historical terms – of Mennonite exceptionalism in North America.

To summarize, what made Mennonites unique was their refusal to envision a world in which a person of faith could also be a full citizen in the world of politics. Symbolically, this distinction took the form of refusing to baptize children into the state church, and of refusing to participate in political life, particularly in the form of military service. This is not to say, I should emphasize, that the practices of adult baptism and conscientious objection ceased to have an inner theological content for Mennonites. That is, if salvation is dependent upon an individual's adult baptism and refusal to bear arms, then in many instances nothing has changed. But the social expression of that content is no longer the same. In other words, the significance of adult baptism was that it made impossible the identity of believer and citizen. Through their accommodation with the demands of citizenship, Mennonites in World War II reestablished that identity. Through doing so, they eliminated the ground on which they had based their exceptionalism, and much of their self-understanding.

Since World War II, Mennonites have struggled with trying to create a form of political participation in which they can maintain their identity as not-quite-citizens. In the second part of this paper, through examining some of the forms in which they have done this, I will discuss the direction which they have led the Mennonite self-understanding of the world of politics.

Part II – Mennonite Politics

Mennonite politics, in the sense of a concern for the 'things of the city', is a recent phenomenon. What began symbolically as a sign of loyalty – participation in the draft – has been accelerated through the actual urbanization of Mennonites, not only into the symbolic 'state' of the United States, but also into the real cities of Chicago, Winnipeg, etc.

24

No longer satisfied and able to remain isolated in small villages, Mennonites have been faced with the realities of metropolitan life and the difficult problem of creating a 'good' city out of the different elements within it.

Because of the tradition of pacifism among Mennonites, the problem is most easily highlighted in relation to Mennonite responses to international conflicts and the politics surrounding international disagreements. This is not to say that Mennonites have not participated in politics at other levels. In fact, their participation has probably been most significant at the community level and in local politics.[17] Nevertheless, in international politics the internal conflict with Mennonite exceptionalism is most acute and therefore most illuminating.

I divide the post-World War II political activity of Mennonites into three periods: pre-Vietnam, Vietnam-era, and post-Vietnam. Prior to the Vietnam War, Mennonites by-and-large were content with their status of full citizens who satisfied their obligations for national service through alternative means.

The Vietnam War, however, provided Mennonites with a new opportunity to show their anti-political roots. Whereas for most American denominations, opposition to the Vietnam War and the Sixties led to a large drop in youth participation, among Mennonites, the tradition of non-resistance was less difficult to reconcile with non-violent activism, and the difference between Anabaptist anti-politics and Vietnam anti-establishment activity was easily glossed over. The result was the establishment within the Mennonite church of more radical politics than within denominations which accepted the war and preached obedience to the state.[18]

Among the various forms which Mennonite opposition to the Vietnam War took, I will discuss two which stand out, and with which I am most familiar. At Bethel College, one of several denominational colleges for Mennonites, students organized a bell ringing demonstration to raise awareness about American casualties of the war. For each American casualty, they rang the school bell once. The demonstration carried on for several days, and received national attention.

At Bethel College, as well, students organized a march to protest the draft. They wrote letters protesting the war and planned to march symbolically to the U.S. Post Office in an adjoining town to mail their letters. In the end, threats of violence from townspeople toward the protesters become acute enough that the march was cancelled in its original form.

Despite the fact that these and other Mennonite activities protesting the Vietnam War were anti-establishment and pacifist, they took the politicization of Mennonites one step further. Fulfilling one's civic duties was no longer enough. It was now important for Mennonites to improve their city, or to try to make it good. As their first experiences with political participation were alongside radicals and utopians, it is not surprising that a vocal part of Mennonite outward expression remained such. From being simply good citizens, Mennonites, along with the other protesters of that era, aspired to change radically the policies of what they now considered their city; in other words, they aspired to rule.

It is interesting to note the dangers which this particular position implies, especially for Anabaptists. As I remarked in the first part of this essay, once Anabaptists refused to accept the established church-state relationship in the sixteenth century, they were faced with two options: utopian theocracy or quietism. With the end of Mennonite quietism brought on by the Vietnam War, it is not surprising that Mennonites would naturally be drawn to manifestations of utopianism, be it secular or otherwise. Because Mennonite utopianism is theologically-based, their politics easily becomes theocratic. Once they begin to think about political issues, they tend to understand their views as theologically inspired. The 'politics' of Jesus easily becomes blended with that of secular utopians.

The radical political movement among Mennonites begun during the Vietnam War has continued into the nineties. Mennonites have been energized to respond politically to the reinstitution of the draft by President Carter in 1979, by the anti-missile protests of the early eighties, by American involvement in Central America, and by the Gulf War. I will briefly look at the issues involved in two of these cases, and the light which it brings to the politicization of Mennonites.

When the Soviet Union invaded Afghanistan in 1979, as a symbolic step to show the alarm which this raised in the West, President Carter reinstated Selective Service registration, which had been abolished along with the draft during the American withdrawal from Vietnam. For Mennonites, this raised the perennial question of the proper non-resistant response. Among the large number of young men who did not bother to register, the Reagan administration, which had since come to power, chose fourteen cases to prosecute in order to try to encourage greater compliance with the law. The fourteen were chosen among those who had not only failed to register, but had also written letters to the Selective Service Administration and other political officials explaining that they refused to participate in the draft, even at the stage of registration, and their reasons for doing so. Among those fourteen, three were Mennonites from Bethel College, the same Mennonite school which had been the scene of Vietnam War protests a decade earlier.

Two of these cases were taken to court. In their trials, both young men offered similar explanations of why they had not registered. They felt that it was against their conscience to take a human life, or even threaten to do so, and they could not participate in President Carter's use of registration as a threat against the Soviet Union. One of them, however, pleaded guilty, admitting that he had knowingly broken the law because his conscience would not allow him to follow it. The other claimed, on technical-legal grounds, that he was not guilty because he was being selectively prosecuted for having written a letter to the Selective Service. This, he believed, was in violation of his First Amendment right to free speech. In the first case, the judge ruled that the Selective Service needed to acknowledge the exceptional religious position of the young man, and required it to print an extra registration card which allowed him to indicate his claim to be a conscientious objector. The Mennonite then registered using this card.[19] In the second case, the Mennonite lost the decision.[20]

The first case, in its essence, represents a reasonably close adherence to the Mennonite position before the Vietnam War. That is, that although one's citizenship is acknowledged and primary duties, such as registration, will be carried out within the system of citizenship, Mennonites continue to demand special treatment because of their beliefs. The argument used is based on Mennonite non-resistance. In this it is consistent with the post-World War II practices of Mennonites.

The second case illustrates the shift which Mennonite political views took during the Vietnam War. This young man no longer asked to be accepted as a citizen despite his refusal to bear arms, but rather argued from within the American Constitution, relying not on the grounds of conscience which are special for Mennonites, but rather using arguments which would apply to any American, regardless of his religious beliefs.

The attitude of the judges in these cases is also worth highlighting. In the first case, the judge acknowledged the arrangements worked out between Mennonites and the government prior to World War II. In effect, he said that within the American Constitution, based on the right to freedom of religion, Mennonites had a right to conscientious objection. In other words, he implied that there was enough flexibility within the American system to incorporate religious radicals fully into American citizenship. Although the Mennonite claimed exceptionalism as the basis of his breaking the law, the judge reinstated him into the ranks of loyal citizens.

In the second case, the judge ruled that the appeal for exceptional treatment based on universal rights is not sufficient. In other words, as long as Mennonites consider themselves exceptional, they are accepted within the American system. But when they try to see themselves as universal, they lose what special status the flexibility of American social policy allows them.

Another opportunity for Mennonites to express themselves politically occurred with the Gulf War in 1990-1991. When U.S. President George Bush decided to take a forceful stand against the Iraqi invasion of Kuwait, the Mennonite response took a number of forms. The leading interpretation in Mennonite churches was the radical one, namely that the war was primarily about oil, not international law. Therefore, Mennonite churches organized activities to indicate their disapproval of a war fought for the American standard of living. Members were encouraged not to use their cars for a day, and to bicycle or walk to church.[21] The most ambitious Mennonite response was the sending of a delegation to Baghdad, under the auspices of an organization called Christian Peacemaker Teams, which was designed to show solidarity with the 'enemy'.

Of special interest for this discussion, however, was the response among Bethel College's students. As a sign of their disapproval of the war, and in an appeal to history, a group of Bethel College students organized a march to the same Post Office which an earlier generation of students had been deterred from reaching. This time the march took place, and the students were able to signal their disagreement with the Bush Administration's policy. What was more significant, however, is that at the same time, another group of Bethel College students decided to organize a counter march. That is, they also demonstrated, not against the build-up in Saudi Arabia, but in favor of the American policy of tough action against Iraq! As far as I am aware, this is the first time that members of a Mennonite body have spoken out in favor of war, or the threat of war.[22]

Conclusion

Throughout their history, Mennonites have tried to remain distinct from political life. Relying on the radical separation implied by their Anabaptist distinction of the Kingdom of God from that of Man, they have made special arrangements with various governments providing them with exceptional rights, most obviously that of conscientious objection. Since the beginning of World War II, however, they have first recognized the state in a more thorough way than previously, and have since begun the process of developing an understanding of politics which they believe to be consistent with Mennonite beliefs.

I believe that these efforts will necessarily fail. When Mennonites emerged from the confines of quietism, they first looked to the left. This was natural, given the similarities between Mennonite understanding and the practice of closely-knit community living, pacifism, and suspicion of government. Once politicization began, however, it was inevitable that Mennonites would begin to align themselves with existing political tradition of all shapes and colors.

The problem with this, for Mennonites, is that, having begun to participate in mainstream politics, be it left or right, it will be increasingly difficult for them to maintain convincingly their exceptional status when it comes to military service. Already in World War II, approximately half of all Mennonites chose not to exercise their privilege of virtually automatic conscientious objector status.[23] Although Mennonites continued to be granted CO status almost automatically during the Vietnam War, and participation in the armed forces declined dramatically from World War II levels, I would argue that the basis on which many Mennonite objectors actually demanded that status had as much to do with secular politics as it did with Anabaptist doctrine. The example of the two Mennonites who refused to register in 1979 should be a lesson. When Mennonites make secular claims for exceptional treatment, they receive a hard hearing. If the exceptional treatment of Mennonites was removed from a future draft policy, it would not surprise me if many young men did not meet the strict requirements of conscience applied to non-historic peace church objector claimants. The occurrence of pro-military demonstrations at Mennonite colleges may hasten this process.

When the Anabaptist movement raised the question of church and state to a new level, Mennonites and other Anabaptists raised the possibility of a political revolution. Five centuries later, their most extraordinary claims – that religion should be voluntary and that violence was not a virtue – have been generally accepted. Christians understanding themselves as Mennonites will not cease to exist in the foreseeable future. But their exceptionalism, particularly in the field of politics, is destined to fade away.

NOTES
1 For a recent example of the sociology of Mennonites and the peace position, see Leo Drieger and Donald B. Kraybill, *Mennonite Peacemaking: From Quietism to Activism*, Scottdale, PA: Herald Press, 1994. For a theological view, see a number of works by Guy F. Hershberger, such as *War, Peace, and Nonresistance*, Scottdale, PA: Herald Press, 1953.
2 C. Henry Smith, *Smith's Story of the Mennonites*, 5th ed. revised and enlarged by Cornelius Krahn, Newton, Kansas: Faith and Life Press, 1981, pp. 8-9. Mennonite scholarship has perhaps been most active in the area of Anabaptist history, and the current historiography on the early Anabaptists is extremely nuanced. This account is necessarily stylized, with apologies to the more exacting Mennonite historians. Two classic texts on Mennonite history are Smith

and C. J. Dyck, *An Introduction to Mennonite History*, Scottdale, Pennsylvania: Herald Press, 1967. For a bibliography of Mennonite scholarship, see Smith.

3   This is the point behind Plato's 'noble lie' in the *Republic*, and also a major source of the power of nationalism. On the latter, see Liah Greenfeld, *Nationalism: Five Roads to Modernity*, Cambridge: Harvard University Press, 1992.

4   For a detailed history of one Mennonite group's interaction with the state and politics, see James Juhnke, *A People of Two Kingdoms: The Political Acculturation of Kansas Mennonites*, Newton, Kansas: Faith and Life Press, 1975.

5   For a comparison of the attitudes of Pennsylvania Mennonites to the state, compared to those of the Quakers and Church of the Brethren, see Roland Bainton, *Christian Attitudes toward War and Peace*, New York, 1960.

6   Smith, p. 284.

7   An exception to this was the vocal pro-German voice of a number of Mennonite newspaper editors during World War I. For a detailed examination of this, see Juhnke, *A People of Two Kingdoms*.

8   See John C. Unruh, *In the Name of Christ: A History of the Mennonite Central Committee and its Services 1920-1951*, Scottdale, Pennsylvania: Herald Press, 1952.

9   See Melvin Gingerich, *Service for Peace: A History of Mennonite Civilian Public Service*, Akron, Pennsylvania: Mennonite Central Committee, 1949, and Guy F. Hershberger, *The Mennonite Church in the Second World War*, Scottdale, Pennsylvania: Herald Press, 1952.

10 The best chronicle of the checkered history of Anabaptists and violence is James M. Stayer, *Anabaptists and the Sword*, new edition, Lawrence, Kansas: Coronado Press, 1976.

11 From Stayer, pp. 119-121. For the complete text of the Confession, see B. Jenny, 'Das Schleitheimer Täuferbekenntnis 1727', *Schaffhauser Beiträge zur vaterländischen Geschichte XXVIII*.

12 See the sixth article of the Schleitheim Confession on the 'Sword'.

13 Although Mennonites began to have difficulties in the U.S. with the Spanish-American War (1898). See Juhnke, p. 58.

14 In Hegel's analysis of civil society and the state (note in *Elements of the Philosophy of Right*, H.B. Nisbit, translator, Allen W. Wood, editor [Cambridge: University Press, 1991], p. 295) Anabaptists (and Quakers) are not full citizens in the state, remaining at the level of civil society.

15 See J.N. Smucker, 'Flags in Churches', *The Mennonite* (1 December, 1953).

16 See A.J. Neuenschwander, 'Representatives from Historic Peace Churches Present Position to Government', *The Mennonite* (9 March, 1937).

17 See Calvin Redekop, *Mennonite Society*, Baltimore: John Hopkins Press, 1989, p. 219.

18 I am indebted to Mark Kroeker for this insight, along with the brief for the Epp selective service case (see below). I should add, however, that Mennonites in general have never been radical in these issues. Mennonites have voted predominantly Republican or Conservative since they began to vote, and have aligned themselves closely with 'conservative' views in the political sphere (see Kaufmann and Lehman, *Anabaptists Four Centuries Later*, Scottdale, Pennsylvania: Herald Press, 1975, and a follow-up study, *The Mennonite*

Mosaic, 1983). Among what Drieger terms 'progressive' Mennonites, and to a large extent among the intellectual circles of Mennonite Colleges, however, a certain radicalization, at least in political issues, has become an accepted part of the mainstream.

19 Telephone conversation with the defendant, Kendal Warkentin (9 October, 1994).

20 See The United States of America v. Charles Robert Epp, 12 June, 1984 (587 F. Supp. 383).

21 *The Mennonite*, 105 (9 October, 1990).

22 Out of fairness, it is necessary to point out that the members of the second march were primarily, if not exclusively, non-Mennonites attending the Mennonite college. I do not believe, however, that this lessens the point. Just as Mennonites in general are becoming diluted into the general population, Mennonite colleges are becoming largely heterogeneous. Students attending a Mennonite college must be considered equal representatives of that institution, regardless of their beliefs. The road from considering attendance and membership in a Mennonite College as not necessarily indicating one's beliefs on peace, to considering attendance and membership in a Mennonite congregation as not necessarily indicating the same, is, in my view, a very short one.

23 Guy F. Hershberger, *The Mennonite Church in the Second World War*, p. 39.

Isolation and Creativity:
The Moravian Church in North America in the Eighteenth and Nineteenth Centuries: Its Cultural Legacy

by Emma Marras, Ph.D

'My kingdom does not belong to this world'   (John 18,36)

'Pay to the Emperor what belongs to the Emperor, and pay to God what belongs to God'   (Mark 12,17)

1. Introduction. The Moravian Identity

MORAVIAN CHURCH STANDS AS THE popular and widely accepted designation in North America for the *Renewed Unitas Fratrum*, which started developing in Saxony in the second decade of the eighteenth century as a reorganization under Pietist influences of the ancient *Unitas Fratrum* dating back to the fifteenth century and whose members were also known as the Bohemian Brethren (or Czech Brethren). The renewal of the *Unitas Fratrum* took place following the encounter between the young Lutheran nobleman Ludwig Nicholas von Zinzendorf (1700-1759), an ardent adept of Pietism, and a small party of some of the few surviving remnants of the *Unitas*, whose families belonged mostly to the Moravian branch of the ancient Church, and who desiring openly to profess their faith and flee persecutions in their homeland, then under Hapsburg jurisdiction, had found refuge on his Saxon estate by Berthelsdorf in Upper Lusatia in 1722.[1]

Due especially to Zinzendorf's instrumental intervention, the *Renewed Unitas Fratrum* soon launched also on an extraordinary missionary program which took it to different countries in Europe, as well as to Greenland, Africa and the New World. Standing as a most ancient Protestant episcopal body, in virtue of its intense and far-reaching missionary activities, the Moravian Church is often rightly considered also as the first truly international Protestant Church.[2] A first party of

32

Moravians reached Georgia in 1734 to settle on the site of part of present-day Savannah. In Georgia, the Moravians hardly ever numbered fifty individuals. By 1740 they had relocated to all-tolerant Pennsylvania, from where they made further settlements in North Carolina. Moravians also went to other colonies, particularly New York and New Jersey, and the Western frontier territories. By the time of the Revolution, their number in the colonies was at least 2,500. Today the Moravian Church in North America has a total membership of approximately 60,000, while total membership world-wide is about 500,000.[3]

It is thus since the first half of the eighteenth century that the Moravian Church, with special European historical roots, has been present in North America. Although they have been active in very limited numbers and usually as separate and often isolated groups within mainstream American society, the Moravians have succeeded in handing down from colonial times to the present their valuable cultural heritage, inclusive of distinctive European traditions, some of them dating back to pre-Reformation times, while also sharing in original fashion in the American experience.

Stressing interdenominational participation and cooperation, the Moravian Church today does not differ greatly in its organization, practices, and doctrines from other Protestant denominations in North America. However, in the eighteenth century and throughout the first half of the nineteenth century it was strongly characterized by a number of features that clearly set it apart from other Protestant Churches in America. The Moravian Church, whose official language was German, had a centralized government for religious as well as administrative and financial affairs at Herrnhut in Germany. The tradition of the ancient *Unitas Fratrum* combined with Pietism and concurred in different degrees to shape the identity of the Church and define its communal brotherly life and its pacifism. With respect to other Protestant denominations in the New World, the *Renewed Unitas Fratrum*, which held Christ as Chief Elder, was particularly Christocentric. The Moravian Brethren were also noted for their missionary work, while since the beginning their level of education and their musical expertise distinguished them among the other German immigrants. The special identity of the Moravian Church in the colonial and national periods was an expression and the result of the Moravians' commitment to lead a saintly life, that is, in Biblical language, to stand 'separate' from the world and its temptations. Separation from mainstream society, which must be viewed primarily as an expression of the religious ideal of the Church, does not necessarily entail isolation and severance of all contacts with the world; proof is the Moravians' aspiration to be of service to the community at large, as best evidenced in their missionary and educational activities and in Zinzendorf's attempt to bring together the different German Protestant Churches during his visit to Pennsylvania in 1741-42.[4]

In cultivating separation from the world, though, according to circumstances and like other religious and non-religious minorities, the Moravians did at times erect walls around their communities against external influences that were deemed to be potentially threatening. This had varied consequences. For example, at first the closed Moravian communities benefited from their self-supporting and self-sufficient economic organization, which made them prosper among the other settlers around them; the Moravians certainly drew some advantages from their arms exemption, a privilege requested and granted them in virtue of their religious conscientious objection to armed conflicts (their 'conscientious scruples against bearing arms'), as the labor contribution of young men was not taken away at any time from the community. This fact itself though soon called on suspicion and attacks from neighbor colonists, which endangered the Moravian position at large and had the communities decide on new measures like paying fines or paying for substitutes, not without some economic loss.[5]

Particularly at critical periods in their early history, the Moravians were actually in a position common somehow to any minority; on more than one occasion they had to find viable solutions between extreme alternatives, when trying to strike a balance between yielding to assimilation into mainstream society and thus benefiting from progress affecting the majority in general, at the cost though of parting, at least to an extent, with their own unique identity, or, on the contrary, resisting assimilation and refusing to conform with the world, at the risk then of incurring into isolation, often synonymous with being the object of more or less subtle discrimination.

No doubt that separation from the world and isolation significantly contributed to hamper the membership of the Moravian Church from growing at a constant pace. This is particularly evident when comparing the pattern of growth of Moravian membership, which slowed down in the first half of the nineteenth century to resume again at the turn of the century, with the expansion of the Methodist Church making its beginnings in England and in the New World precisely at the same time as the Moravian Church and soon becoming one of the very largest Protestant denominations in North America. The different reasons that seriously prevented Moravian membership from growing numerically are discussed by Bishop John Taylor Hamilton, of Bethlehem, who wrote a documented history of his Church at the close of the last century when the *Renewed Unitas Fratrum* in North America had achieved autonomy with respect to Church authorities at Herrnhut, in Europe, following the General Synod of 1857. Hamilton refers in particular to the neutrality of the Church (which is an implicit criticism on his part of some aspects of Moravian pacifism), an 'exaggerated conception of the headship of Christ over the Church' which had resulted in resort to the lot to decide on such vital issues as the appointment of religious leaders or the choice of marriage partners (somehow limiting therefore the role of individual responsibility), and the protracted use of German in religious services; Hamilton includes as well some remarks on the excessive fear on the part of the Church to incur the charge of proselytism.[6]

Nevertheless, even though separation and isolation were an obstacle to the increase in the membership of the Church, the efforts of the Moravians in the New World to preserve their ancient religious faith and their very attachment to a peculiar set of practices all helped in making it possible for their communities to pass on to this day a most valuable cultural, material and spiritual legacy, carefully handed down and even enriched upon from generation to generation.

'Small is beautiful!', one is indeed tempted to exclaim! American fashion, when considering the contrast between the numerical presence of the Moravians, who have represented by all standards a small minority within American society at large – and whose number was at times practically negligible, as in the instance of their first settlement in Georgia – and the significance of their cultural contribution to the American reality.

Moravian contributions to American life do include some notable examples, particularly in the fields of architecture, sacred music, and education; the Moravians have also left a lasting mark on American religious thought and practice, as witnessed by their lovefeast services, their religious songs, their Christmas and Easter celebrations, that were soon adopted by other denominations. The degree to which the first Moravians interacted with and even influenced the Wesley brothers, who founded Methodism, is an aspect of eighteenth century Moravian history which deserves consideration, particularly with regard to the action of some of the major Moravian figures, like Zinzendorf and Augustus Gottlieb Spangenberg (1704-1792).[7] Furthermore, the flourishing closed Moravian communities of Pennsylvania and North Carolina, with their special 'general economy' system, represented conspicuous instances typical of the eighteenth century religious utopian communal (or collectivistic) experience, as Arthur Bestor has accurately highlighted in his important study *Backwood Utopias: The Sectarian origins of the Owenian Phase of Communitarian Socialism in America, 1663-1829*.[8] Pacifism, entailing a complex attitude to issues of war and peace, is another significant aspect of Moravian life; it has been studied extensively and in detail by Peter Brock who also indicates how Moravian pacifism differs from the uncompromising pacifism of the historical Peace Churches.[9] Utopian communal living and pacifism are relevant cultural phenomena, most often tightly interconnected, that have developed in original fashion within American society.

An intense missionary activity among different Indian nations is an additional characteristic of Moravian history in the eighteenth and early nineteenth centuries, as witnessed in the contents of such works as the *History of the Mission of the United Brethren among the Indians of North America* (1794), *Transactions of the Moravian Historical Society* (1888), the *Records of the Moravians in North Carolina* (1913).[10] Moravian sources, that deserve perhaps to be better known than they are at present, can certainly concur to widen our knowledge and understanding of special aspects of the history of native Eastern American Indians in the eighteenth and nineteenth centuries and their interaction with the white settlers.

It is also somehow typical of Moravian history that two important urban centers like Bethlehem, Pennsylvania with a population of about 60,0000, known especially for its steel and ship building industry that developed at the beginning of our century, and Winston-Salem, North Carolina with a growing population of over 140,000, known world-wide for its tobacco and cigarette industry, have both actually grown out of two small eighteenth century Moravian closed communal settlements, German-speaking in origin and at least until the first years of the nineteenth century, with non-Moravians not allowed to settle on the communal land, which belonged to the Unity.[11] The Moravian presence is still especially felt today in Pennsylvania and North Carolina, where the two self-governing provinces of the Moravian Church in the United States, the Northern and the Southern, have their seats in Bethlehem and Winston-Salem respectively.

Perhaps the most tangible signs nowadays of the industrious and creative presence of the Moravians in North America since colonial times are the beautiful sets of buildings making use of local material and dating from the eighteenth century found in Moravian historic sites in Pennsylvania and North Carolina. In Bethlehem, austere stone structures in impressive Germanic style and reflecting past communal organization date from the 1740's and 1750's, like the Widow's House (1742), the Bell House (1745), the old Chapel (1752); other examples of Moravian architecture are to be found notably at Nazareth, the first Moravian settlement in Pennsylvania (Nazareth Hall, 1755, Whitefield House, 1740, now a museum), and nearby Lititz with Linden Hall, the Moravian school for girls founded in 1794.

The Bethlehem Bach Choir, organized in 1898, and numbering over 160 members who are Bethlehem area residents, speaks for the centuries long Moravian interest in sacred and choral music: as early as 1742, that is one year after it was first settled, Bethlehem housed its first 'singstunde', while the 'Collegium musicum' which was founded in 1744 and continued until 1820 when it was replaced by the Philharmonic Society, started performing parts of several oratorios. Bethlehem Moravians also imported to America from Europe the first copies of Haydn's quartets and symphonies and are to be credited with the first American performances of Handel's *The Creation* and *The Seasons*.[13] Benjamin Franklin himself noted the quality of the music performed in 1756 in the Church at Bethlehem, where flutes, oboes, French horns and trumpets were used with the organ at a much earlier date than in other parts of the colonies (in New England, for instance, the use of French horns and oboes was first mentioned only in 1761 and 1789 respectively).

Bethlehem also significantly testifies to the Moravian tradition in education as it houses in particular the Moravian Academy (the successor of the school for girls founded in Germantown by Benigna Zinzendorf when visiting Pennsylvania with her father in 1742), Moravian Theological Seminary (opened at Nazareth in 1807, and finally moved to Bethlehem in 1858), Moravian Preparatory School, and Moravian Seminary for Girls, in nearby Green Pond.[14]

In restored historic Old Salem, now part of Winston-Salem, the communal buildings in red brick and clay are neatly ordered along Main Street and around Salem Square. The tile-roofed buildings in Old Salem, dating from mid-eighteenth and early nineteenth centuries were first restored in the late 1920's and early 1930's, then again most recently after the storm of 1980.[15] With their characteristic large wood beams, their stone steps and hooded doorways, and other typical details, such as door handles, locks and shutter fasteners, the buildings recall the European origins of the early settlers who founded the community in 1766 and reflect its organization into 'choirs' according to age, sex and marital status, as well as its pattern of growth (e.g. the Brother's House, 1769, the Single Sisters' House, 1785, the Boys' School, 1794, the Miksch Tobacco Shop, 1771, the Community Store, 1775, the Tavern, 1784, the Home Moravian Church, 1800, which replaced the Gemeinhaus of 1766 as a place of worship). God's Acre is the compelling site of Salem cemetery, with row upon row of identical white tomb stones in separate burial plots for the men, the women, and the little ones of the community. As in Bethlehem, in Old Salem, Moravian customs and traditions are revived all year round, but especially at Christmas, with the Lighting of the Star and the Candle Tea, and at Easter with the celebrated outdoor Sunrise Service in God's Acre.[16]

Salem also houses two unique educational institutions for young women, Salem College and Salem Academy, which both grew out of the Salem School for Girls founded in 1772. Salem has in fact continued to provide first-rate education for young women with no interruption since then. With its historical Moravian buildings, including the Single Sisters' House, and its fifty-six acre grounds, largely wooded with native forest trees, the Salem campus is particularly attractive. Among the architectural structures on Salem campus, Main Hall, dominating Salem Square since 1856 with its white Doric portico, is of relevance when tracing the development and successive transformations of Moravian identity.[17] Its classic style attests to how by the middle of the nineteenth century the closed community of the earlier days had definitely opened up to external influences and was participating in national life in every way.

The Moravian Music Foundation, founded in 1956, gathers an impressive collection of musical compositions, many in manuscript form; some are copies of great European composers, including Haydn and Handel, while some were written by Moravian composers, notably John Frederick Peter (1746-1813) who went to America in 1770; John Frederick Peter composed chamber music and served as organist and director of music for the Moravian Church at Salem from 1780 to 1790.[18]

The legacy of the past surfaces in the Moravian tradition that continues to the present also in the poetry of H.D. (Hilda Doolittle, 1886-1961), born in Bethlehem, of Moravian stock on her mother's side, and best known for her Imagist and Modernist poems and her intense involvement and friendship with other great Modernist writers, including Ezra Pound, Marianne Moore, William Carlos Williams. Ellen Wolle, H.D.'s mother, came from one of the original Moravian families who founded the Bethlehem community in the eighteenth century. Moravian traditions naturally nurtured the poet's childhood. Her Moravian identity reappears most explicitly in her later works, particularly *The Gift* (1941-43); significantly, one of her later texts, her unpublished *The Mystery* (1949-1951), is dedicated to Count Zinzendorf.[19]

The complex cultural identity of the Moravian Church has been characterized by its creative response in the face of its peculiar position vis-à-vis mainstream society since colonial times. Moravian creativity is also an expression of the different traditions that have converged to shape the present reality of the Moravian Church, starting with the tradition of separation from the world introduced at the time of the ancient *Unitas Fratrum*, which Pietism reinforced three centuries later.

2. The *Unitas Fratrum* until 1722. Its Vicissitudes. Separation from the World throughout Centuries. The Herrnhut Community

In the course of its transformations throughout its centuries-long history, from the fifteenth century to the early eighteenth, the *Unitas Fratrum* underwent several influences that were to leave lasting marks on its life and later reappear in the *Renewed Unitas Fratrum* of the eighteenth century. (e.g., communal life, role of women, emphasis on education, cultivation of sacred music, interaction with other religious bodies). A pattern of growth followed by hardship, persecution, and decline until its renewal under Pietist influences can be traced in the history of the ancient Unitas, which the pattern of development of the *Renewed Unitas* in North America loosely parallels.

In the New World, the Moravians were at first present with small communities which scarcely numbered a hundred individuals (in 1740, for example, Bethlehem, then the major Moravian community in the New World, counted about one hundred and forty settlers); in a few decades the Moravians multiplied, and by the beginning of the Revolution they had reached prosperity; their slow Americanization process, however, tended crucially to hamper their normal growth until roughly the middle of the nineteenth century. By the end of the nineteenth century, though, the Moravian Church in America was undergoing a renewal process as it assessed its identity as an episcopal Protestant evangelical denomination, conscious of its limited membership when compared with other Protestant denominations, like the Baptists and the Methodists, but also of its special cultural identity while favoring interdenominational communication, so that whereas in the past there had been at times occasional frictions and rivalry, particularly with the Baptists and the Methodists, the Moravians were now actively interacting with other religious bodies. And by the beginning of the twentieth century, the Moravian Church started stressing its position as the guardian of a valuable legacy which had been brought forth from Europe, enriched upon at the time of its isolation in the eighteenth century, and then put to the test in the following years as the Moravians were confronting their American national identity. In the second half of our century, the Moravian Church has been intent on treasuring its novel identity, resulting from both its awareness of its American nature and its responsibility in continuing to make an original contribution on the national as well as international scene, by emphasizing cultivating precisely some of those aspects of its life that through its history have accounted for its difference from other religious bodies, such as its tradition in theological studies, its role in education, its belief in peaceful negotiations to settle conflicts, its emphasis on church music, the up-dated study of its impressive archives.[20]

Moravian sources often point to the very ancient East European origins of the old *Unitas Fratrum*, referring ideally to Cyril and Methodius, though the *Unitas Fratrum* first developed as such in Central Europe in the Late Middle Ages, as an off-shoot of the Hussite Church, the national Church of Bohemia, which had been expanding after the death of the Protestant martyrs Jan Hus and Jerome of Prague, the religious leaders burnt at the stake at the Council of Constance in 1415 and 1416 respectively.[21] In 1457 a group of Hussites retired at Kunwald in the mountains East of Prague with Gregory Rokyana, the nephew of the utraquist Bishop of Prague, forming an association known as *Jednota Bratrska* (Unity of the Law of Christ), intending to carry forth in thorough fashion the religious program of Jan Huss, assessing total separation from Rome, in contrast therefore with the national church of Bohemia. In 1467 the 'Unity' gave life to the *Unitas Fratrum* and as they became then strongly influenced by the radical tendencies of their new leader Peter Chelcicky (1390 ca-1460 ca), the Brethren saw the State as a heathen institution and tended to identify Christian teaching with non resistance to evil.[22] Their literal interpretation of Scriptures (in particular their reading of the Sermon on the Mount), which had them stress Christian fellowship in general, had also the first Brethren refuse to take oaths and bear arms. It was at that time that the Brethren contacted the Waldenses to assure the establishment of their own episcopacy.

Following the radical and uncompromising leadership of Peter Chelcičky, which in the end led to sterile results, opposing as it did innovations and external influences, with Luke of Prague (*Lukas Prazsky*, d. 1528) the *Unitas* moved towards a more moderate position: it accepted an increasing number of laymen and started interacting more and more with the cultural and political world. As representatives of all ranks of society were encouraged to join, the nobility could maintain ownership of its estates, while the different trades and professions became regulated according to Christian principles. The education and spiritual upbringing of the young was a major concern of the *Unitas*, which also cared to put matrons (*magistrae*) in charge of young girls. The Brethren were noted particularly for their printing presses, at Mlada Boleslav and Lytamyl, which helped spread their doctrines even outside Bohemia and Moravia. Their interest in church music, to express the faith of the people, led them to print the first Protestant hymnal in 1501.

Widely travelled through Europe – in 1498 he was in Italy where he met the Piedmont Waldenses – Luke of Prague especially contributed to the great intellectual and cultural development of the *Unitas* on the eve of the Reformation, when the *Unitas* counted four hundred churches in Bohemia and Moravia. And the growing popularity and influence of the *Unitas* even led King Vladislav II of the Jagellonians to oppose it declaring it a *picard* (or *beghard*) sect in 1508.[23]

Even though on doctrinal grounds the *Unitas* tended to encline towards Calvin's teachings, as Moravian historians recall, which better conformed with its own disciplined way of life, it also related with the Lutherans, under whose influence it abandoned celibacy for its pastors (as well as its earlier uncompromising pacifism) and started to undergo a process of secularization of some sort.[24] And when in 1526 the Hapsburg dynasty replaced the Jagellonians under whose rule the *Unitas* had been allowed to prosper, members from the ranks of the nobility were instrumental in having the church take side with the Lutherans to oppose the new monarch. The Lutheran defeat at Smalcalda in 1548 set the beginning of a long period of trial and persecution for the Brethren who were expelled from Bohemia. Many of them moved to Poland thus giving life to a third branch of the *Unitas*, while Moravia, where the Brethren were spared persecution thanks to the intervention of the Diet, became the center of the Church.

At this time in its history, the Church saw to it that its younger members be instructed in the major centers of Protestant culture. The Church came to excel in its intellectual, scientific and literary activities, as shown by the work of John Blahoslav (1523-1571), while its hymnals were used in Germany itself; the famous illuminated Bible of Kralice dates from that period. The memory of this literary production was preserved in the first Moravian communities in Pennsylvania; it is this production which inspired part of the later writings of Hilda Doolittle.

In the second half of the sixteenth century and the first decades of the following century, the *Unitas* did undertake efforts, *albeit* short-lived ones, in order to bring about cooperation with other evangelical Protestant bodies to withstand Counter-Reformation attacks; the Brethren united with the Hussites and the Lutherans of Bohemia in 1575 and again in 1609 on the basis of the Brethren's own Bohemian confession of 1575 (which followed the *Hapsburg litterae majestatis* on religious freedom). Despite these attempts at a united front, divisions were hardly overcome. During the Thirty Years' war, the *Unitas* underwent harsh persecutions, and became almost extinct following the Protestant defeat at the battle of the White Mountain in 1620. The surviving members of the *Unitas* either went into exile or practiced underground. Though it was by then a crushed and scattered Church, in the seventeenth century the *Unitas* continued to plead for religious freedom, its activities centering mostly in Lezno, Poland. During this most difficult period in its history, at the head of the *Unitas* was John Amos Comenius (*Jan Amos Komensky*, 1592-1670), best-known for his work as an educator and philosopher. Born at Nivnice in Moravia, Comenius taught in the *Unitas* schools in Poland (at Fulnek, notably); his fame called him to England and Sweden; from 1655 to his death he lived in Amsterdam.[25] Today Comenius is remembered especially as a pioneer in teaching; education, he insisted (ahead of his time), should be imparted to children, starting at a very young age, and young people of all social classes and both sexes. Some sources indicate that when in England he was also offered the Presidency of Harvard College, to which he preferred remaining in Europe to care for his Church. In his last writings Comenius, who left a great number of works in Latin, German and Czech, lamented the tragic fate of his Church, but also expressed his hope that a 'hidden seed' of the *Unitas* faith may nevertheless keep growing in his native Moravia.

The spread of Pietism which developed in the Lutheran Church at the beginning of the seventeenth century proved providential to the revival of Comenius' Church. It was the evangelical itinerant preacher Christian David, born in Sentfelden in Moravia in 1690 and a carpenter by trade, who first encouraged surviving members of the *Unitas* to leave their land, by then under Hapsburg rule, and seek freedom of worship on Zinzendorf's estate in nearby Saxony in 1722, which was to be the first step towards the renewal of the *Unitas* that took place in the following years. On Zinzendorf's estate at Berthelsdorf, at the foot of the Hutberg, the Moravians immediately started erecting their small community which was named Herrnhut (in the Lord's watch). In 1724, they were joined by other young Moravians from Kunwalde and Zaichtenthal also influenced by David's preaching and who had intended as well to revive the ancient *Unitas*.[26]

Raised in a Pietist environment and educated at Pietist institutions, Zinzendorf intended to promote a sort of self-help community within the greater Lutheran Church body, according to the Pietist principle of *ecclesiolae in ecclesia*.[27] However, the spirit of the *Unitas* came to prevail over the Lutheran component in the Herrnhut community, and in 1735 Comenius's nephew, Daniel Ernst Jablonski, who retained the *Unitas* episcopate, consecrated the Moravian David Nitschmann; in 1737 Zinzendorf himself received episcopal consecration from Jablonski and Nitschmann, which suggests how the *Renewed Unitas* was starting to establish its own separate status, distinct from that of the Lutheran Church, and looking forward to its own future development.

3. The *Renewed Unitas Fratrum*. Its Beginnings in the New World

Like its counterparts in Europe and, starting in 1734, in the New World, Herrnhut was structured as a religious socio-economic self-sufficient community with a tendency to abolish the principle of individual property, as in the early Christian communities. Different arts and crafts were present in the community, which had also its own apothecary. Herrnhut, on the other hand, was also known from the start for its tutors and instructors, usually trained in Pietist institutions, and some of whom were even called to the Court at Dresden, which suggests that the Herrnhut experiment in communal living was regarded with sympathy and con-sideration in some specific socio-political circles at least, despite official opposition to Zinzendorf that was also beginning to develop.[28]

While the presence of several skilled artisans contributed to Herrnhut's growing prosperity, the community also received significant financial support from a number of Pietist influenced members of the aristocracy and other sympathizing moneyed members of society, in different parts of Europe, given Zinzendorf's cosmopolitan ties.

As Herrnhut was fast expanding, its spirit reached out even beyond Europe, when Zinzendorf became interested in missionary work following his chance meeting in Dresden with a fugitive African slave from the West Indies. A special desire to preach to the Indians of North America had Zinzendorf and his associates make arrangements to establish settlements in the New World. Especially at times when some friction was arising with the Lutheran authorities, a passage overseas to the New World could also represent an opportunity for emigration for part of the Herrnhutters, considering the pressing need to provide for the great number of refugees of diverse Protestant origins that kept joining the communal experiment. In the short or long run, it would not prove feasible to keep accommodating all of them, and as in the case of the party of Schwenckfelders who arrived in 1726, it would even prove inconvenient to have them remain in the Saxon community permanently.[29] In addition, Zinzendorf and his associates, particularly Spangenberg ('Brother Joseph') and George Bönisch, of German stock, were concerned with the fate of the many German immigrants – it is estimated that there were about one hundred thousand – in the English colonies living for the most part in a state of quasi spiritual anarchy, due especially to the lack of German-speaking pastors that could provide for their spiritual and religious well-being.

Meanwhile, as his position in the Herrnhut community came to interfere with his hereditary rank and his charges in the court at Dresden, by 1736 Zinzendorf had to leave Saxony to return only at the end of his life. Outside of Saxony, though, he continued to operate in favor of the *Renewed Unitas* from his London-based headquarters, travelling widely also in Northern Europe and overseas. His connections in England, especially his friendship with James Ogglethorpe, dating from their youth, facilitated the acquisition of land in the colonies, first in Georgia, the original destination of the Schwenckfelders, then in Pennsylvania (where the *Renewed Unitas* acquired in 1735 the Nazareth property which had first been in the name of George Whitefield), and North Carolina where the 99,000 acres of the Wachovia settlement were purchased from Lord Granville in 1753.

It was at the time of their first crossing to Georgia in 1734, on the ship during their journey from Pennsylvania to Georgia, that their fellow-passenger John Wesley noticed the Moravians – 'the Germans', as he recorded it – for their exemplary behavior and fortitude, as they gathered in prayer during a great storm.[30] So strong was their ideal of communion and devotional unity permeating the life of the eighteenth century Moravians that even on board the vessels carrying them to America, as on the Unity-owned *Irene*, they maintained their devotional organization forming actual 'sea congregations'. And when revisiting the Moravian past, the Moravian 'sea-congregations' praising the Prince of Peace on their vessels carrying them across the Atlantic summon up the images of small islands of ideal Christian worship, moving across the wilderness of the Ocean. In reaching the English colonies, the Brethren would gather in their communities that stood like islands of saintly life, human resource-fulness and culture amidst the wilderness of the backwoods.

Choosing to live in seclusion, as it were, to spend all for their religious faith, and to avoid mundane distractions did not prevent the Brothers and Sisters from relating to the social reality around them. They did so with their work on the community, which produced goods and services, from which other fellow colonists could also benefit and which would have hardly been available otherwise, but most especially when sharing the Word of the Lord Christ and ministering pastoral care. In their role as 'visitors' and 'fishers', in their itinerant preaching, and in their mission-ary activity, though, they were instructed not to come into conflict with other pastors and preachers, and to work towards sincere and heart-felt rather than numerous conversions, which is an indication of how the early Moravians conceived of their mode of association with the world. Their pattern of religious preaching was in contrast, for example, with the mass gatherings led by George Whitefield and his dramatic, quasi-histrionic public performances.

If the Moravians actually succeeded in entertaining good relationships especially with the Friends and the Anglicans and Presbyterians, they also avoided in principle and in fact to oppose established government author-ities. To this effect, they obtained official recognition to practice their pacifist ideal first from the English Parliament – and successively from the young United States' government.

Moravian leaders cultivated good understanding with the colonial authorities and later with the representatives of the new Republic. Moravian leader John Ettwein (1721-1802), for example, first visited Governor Tryon of North Carolina in 1766, the following year Governor Tryon visited the Salem community, and Governor Josiah Martin did so in 1772, while in 1791 the community was to receive the visit of President George Washington.[31] Adelaide Fries has indicated how government authorities valued positively the conduct of the Moravians and the services they rendered to the community at large, despite the trumped up charges they were at times the victims of because of jealousy and suspicion due to the comparatively flourishing economy in their settlements.[32]

4. Moravian Communities in North America in the Eighteenth and Early Nineteenth Centuries. The General Economy. Conscientious Scruples to Bearing Arms. Missions Among the Indians. Bilingual Identity

The socio-economic semi-communitarian organization known as 'General Economy' and a refusal to bear arms and take judicial oaths strongly defined the identity of the early Moravian communities in North America. Such characteristics revived exemplary practices of the first Christian communities which had been resumed at the beginning of the *Unitas Fratrum* in fourteenth century Central Europe and were adopted again at Herrnhut.

American Moravian historians stress that the General Economy was intended to be only of a limited duration in North America and was planned to promote cooperation among the settlers and missionaries, so that the new communities could be better equipped emotionally and financially in view of the rough beginnings they were expected to face.[33]

The General Economy represented a community of labor and finance that made possible the exceptionally rapid development of the first settlements. The Brothers and Sisters received communal housing and a subsistence wage in exchange of their labor. Hamilton explains that: 'No private business was transacted, but the manufactures and trades were carried on for the benefit of the church organization under responsible committees'.[34] Hamilton also suggests that it was 'a system Spartan in its rigor, and yet voluntarily submitted to for Christ's sake'.[35]

Hamilton indicates how the system of the General Economy had allowed the first communities to prosper, recalling that by 1747, when they supported about fifty missionaries and itinerant preachers, Bethlehem and Nazareth counted 'several farms and thirty-two different industries', stressing that 'no town in the interior of Pennsylvania could so sufficiently supply all kinds of wants'.[36] Likewise at Salem, for instance, the Tavern, known for its cleanliness and good cooking, offered a service well appreciated by travellers journeying from several miles around, particularly in the difficult years of the Revolution.

In Pennsylvania, the strict General Economy system lasted until 1761 while in North Carolina it lasted until 1771, when the Tobacco Shop of Matthew Miksch in Salem became the first privately owned building on the Wachovia Moravian settlement. The Church, however, continued to own all community land and property not in the hands of individual members, with only Church members allowed to settle on communal land; the community Elders were entitled to reprimand members whose behavior did not comply with community standards and requirements. Only in mid-nineteenth century did the Moravian religious authorities cease to have control over the personal, social and economic activities carried on by the community members; this was a final step towards the full secularization and Americanization of the Moravian communities.

The choir system, at one time in effect in the ancient *Unitas*, was a special characteristic of Moravian communal life. The members of the community were separated into different choirs according to age, sex, and marital status. In Salem, for instance, young boys and unmarried men lived and worked in the Single Brothers' House. The House was complete with kitchen and dining-room on the ground-floor (or first basement), and a cellar for perishable goods in the sub basement; on the street-floor were the workshops and industries and a small chapel. The young Brothers learnt different arts and trades under the supervision of master craftsmen, while the Supervisor of the House cared for their moral and religious education. The dress code itself also pointed to the choir organization. To-day, for example, as they are greeted to a vivid reconstruction of early Moravian community life, visitors can notice hostesses of different age groups representing the Moravian Sisters, wearing eighteenth century simple dresses, with the color of the ribbons on their small white caps indicating their status in the community, pink for single women, blue for married women, white for widows, and bright red for little girls.[37]

The closed communities functioning according to the principle of the General Economy represented a form of isolation from the world that helped the Moravians avoid being subjected to negative worldly influences that would distract them from their religious and spiritual commitment.

Such isolation also contributed to promote economic autonomy and a material prosperity that was conducive for the Moravians to focus on their own spiritual and cultural heritage. For they could develop undisturbed activities that were encouraged by Pietist teachings and relating to traditions, even long-lost ones, of the ancient *Unitas Fratrum*, silenced during the years of persecution, like those connected with their role as educators, and their cultivation of sacred music, additional to expanding and intensifying their missionary activity to which community surplus income was devoted.

Together with their ideal of brotherly love, which was expressed in communal life, the first Moravians brought to America from the Old World their love for peace. Their vision of peace inspired their naming of the new centers, like Salem in the North Carolina Wachovia settlement, but also, for example, Friedberg and Friedland founded in Wachovia in 1773 and 1775, or some of the mission stations founded by David

Zeisberger, *Friedenshutten* (Tents of Peace) in 1765, on the North branch of the Susquehanna, at the suggestion of Chief Papunhank, a convert to the Moravian faith, *Friedenstadt* (City of Peace), in 1770, on the Allegheny, on a site first reached by an expedition of sixteen canoes, Salem in 1779, on the Ohio.[38]

And whereas from the start the observance of the General Economy system was planned to be of a limited duration, at the beginning the commitment to non violence was intended to be a lasting one and special steps were undertaken that were supposed to safeguard the Moravians' right to conscientious objection to bearing arms and taking oaths.[39]

Yet the Moravians who had been moved to go to the New World by their desire to serve the Lord of Peace, had almost from the start to face the demands of the world and pay their tribute to government authorities. Initially, in Georgia, the pacifism of the Moravians proved of an absolute, unconditional nature, so much so that it was a major reason for their going to Pennsylvania when war was threatening on the Florida border. Such pacifism, though, was short-lived. And the first Moravians, in receiving official assurance of the liberty to practice their faith, which they finally obtained in 1749, also accepted their obligations toward the established government, as stated in the Act of Parliament that in fact, as Adelaide Fries points out, granted them special privileges, that could be compared to those enjoyed by the Church of England: 'Several of the said Brethren do consciously scruple the taking of an Oath, bearing arms, or personally serving in any military capacity, though willing to contribute sums of money as a reasonable compensation for such services which shall be necessary for the defense and support of His Majesty's Person and Government'.[40] The special conditions of frontier life in America, the rise of hostilities during the French and Indian War (Seven Years' War, which ended in 1763), and the unforeseen events of the American Revolution would hasten the beginning of the Americanization and secularization process of the Moravian Church with regard to its commitment to non-violence.[41]

In Pennsylvania, where women and children were present on the Moravian communities, as had not been the case in the pioneer days in Georgia, at the time of the French and Indian War defensive measures were organized by Spangenberg himself who, when in Georgia, had diplomatically avoided, on health grounds, to appear at drills as required by the British local authorities. Although they avoided to bear arms, the Pennsylvania and North Carolina Moravians were instrumental in protecting the Northern and Western borders; palisades and forts were erected, night watches organized, and converted Indians helped by going on reconnaissance tours.

Despite their active participation in the defense of the threatened colonial front and despite their help as intermediaries, which was instrumental in solving conflicts between colonial authorities and hostile Indian chiefs, the Moravians were nevertheless usually regarded with some suspicion because of their privilege of arms exemption. Indians allied with the British also resented the Moravians whose influence prevented converted Indians from following them on the war path.

Conscientious objection (and oath taking, following the passing of the Test Act of 1776-1777 requiring a repudiation of loyalty to the King) became an increasingly crucial issue around 1775, when the political situation was such that – Adelaide Fries recalls – for many of the colonists it could be summarized in the paradoxical recommendation: 'Be loyal to the King and oppose his government'.[42]

At the beginning of the revolution, like most Friends and like the representatives of the German sects in general, John Ettwein (1721-1802), the Moravians' leader at the time, tended to favor the Loyalist position. His competence, his courage, his 'strong good sense', though, had long won him the respect of several Patriot leaders, including Henry Laurens and George Washington. Particularly under the influence of Hans Christian Alexander von Schweinitz, who was on the governing board of the Church, Ettwein himself soon came to understand the Patriots' cause. The Church did resist direct military involvement for its members; while it disapproved of paying for substitutes, it did help individual Brothers pay heavy fines in commutation of participation in the militia drills – a number of young Brothers were also imprisoned for refusing to serve in the militia.

The Church did in fact support the Continental army in non-violent ways. While heavy fines were paid when required, when members of the Church did bear arms, which happened consistently in New York, they were not severely sanctioned by the Church. In Wachovia, starting in 1775, Brother Bagge practically acted as a disguised purchasing agent for the Continental forces. The Moravians also accepted paper currency in payment for their services. Bethlehem housed the general hospital of the Continental army from December 1776 to March 1777, and from September 1777 to June 1778, with Ettwein himself as Chaplain.[43]

Certainly the approach to pacifism among the North American Moravians, who have been present in different parts of the territory and holding different positions in their communities, has not been an overall homogenous one. A sort of dichotomy can be detected in the Moravian views on military service. Even though the Moravian leaders clearly did not intend to resist established state authorities, the official Church policy long remained firmly opposed to having any of the Moravians serve in any military capacity; nevertheless, many of them, particularly the younger generations, did not actually object to it.[44]

A similar conflict of opinion can in fact be identified when discussing the Moravian approach to slavery. In the 1840's, for example, in the Salem community in North Carolina, there were instances of Negro slave work in privately-owned businesses that did not officially declare it, although this went against Church policy and was condemned by the Church Elders who were at the time still entitled to retain control over all community affairs.[45] Such occurrences can be viewed as a further aspect of the secularization process of the community that went accelerating in the ante-bellum years.

While it is important to discuss it in the context of the process of the Americanization of the *Renewed Unitas Fratrum* in the United States, Moravian pacifism, though, also had tragic consequences that should not be overlooked, for repeatedly Moravian converts and Moravian missionaries holding to their peace testimony, usually away from the major centers of Moravian influence, were victims of violence – and true martyrs of peace.

The most salient episode of this sort was the Gnadenhutten massacre of 1782 in the Tuscarawas valley; following mistreatment and plundering by British troops and the summoning of Zeisberger and other missionaries to Detroit as spies, ninety Christian Indians and six visitors were murdered in cold blood by American militia men distrusting Moravian neutrality. And on other occasions, as during the war of 1812, when following their victory at the battle of the Thames, by Detroit, in October 1813 American troops burnt the prosperous Fairfield mission which had served as a hospital for the British, the Moravians' attachment to their ideal, unpopular though highly commendable, was misunderstood and called for discrimination against them.[46]

The strong missionary impulse typical of the *Renewed Unitas Fratrum* resulted in the remarkable accomplishments of the Moravians among the Indians in North America. In the colonial period, Indian converts were at times practically almost as many as the Moravians of European stock.[47] The early Moravians' dedication to missionary activity, their desire to share the Word of Christ the Savior with those who did not yet know Him, certainly characterized their response to the Indian reality with regards to the tolerant and all-respectful, equalitarian approach of the Friends, and on the other hand the oligarchic and superior attitude of the Puritan position which even demonized the red men. The Moravian missionary activity stands as a very special aspect of the North American cultural experience, as it represents an exception in the North American world of the eighteenth and early nineteenth centuries. King Philip's War of 1675 had practically put an end to English missions among the Indians started by John Eliot (1605-1690) in New England.

David Zeisberger and the other Moravian missionaries of the first days learnt to speak the native American languages and to know and respect the area where they were to operate. In addition to their role as explorers, they performed a mediating role as cultural intermediaries and they helped to the non-violent furthering of the inevitable colonization process.[48]

The use of German resulting in the marked bilingual identity of the early Moravian communities in the New World adds to the exceptional character of the *Renewed Unitas Fratrum* in North America and to its configuration as a minority religious body.

The first generations of American Moravians were accustomed to preach either in German or in English, depending on the audience they were addressing. In 1772, for example, Spangenberg wrote that in Philadelphia where the two congregations (of the Brethren of 'the English and of the German nation') had united, divine service was held in both languages by turns.[49] The use of German, though, for hymn singing and religious celebrations (as opposed to preaching) became a major factor preventing the growth of church membership. The persistence of German into the nineteenth century for religious services and official documents was a sign of the centralized government of the Church with its seat at Herrnhut in Germany which came to an end only in mid-nineteenth century.[50]

When at the beginning of our century Adelaide Fries undertook to translate into English the Records of the Moravians of North Carolina, it was an assessment on the part of the Moravian communities of their own heritage, which had flourished during their decades of isolation, and one which is significant not only for the Moravian Church, but also statewide, and nationwide. Ultimately, as the Moravian documents include an uninterrupted and insightful account of historical events since colonial times, their scholarly and cultural value is international.

5. Salem College. The Moravian Outlook to the Future: Treasuring the Vision of the Founding Brothers and Sisters

With its achievements in women's education, Salem College clearly illustrates how the Moravians have sought solutions enabling them to retain their rich identity while coexisting with majority groups and accounting for realities different from their own; looking for such solutions has also made it possible for the Moravians to integrate into American cultural life and even concur to revitalize some sectors of society at large by relying on their own special skills and cultural traditions.

As Dr. Howard Rondthaler, Salem's President from 1909 to 1949, remarked, the school, following in the Moravian tradition, has been 'seeking to retain those things which are good, yet also trying to keep abreast with current trends of importance, so that they (the students) will be equipped to meet the problems which inevitably come with tomorrow'.[51]

Though it started awarding diplomas replacing earlier certificates of scholarship in 1878 and Bachelor of Arts degrees in 1890 later than other female institutions, (notably Mount Holyoke in Massachusetts, founded by Mary Lyon in 1836, Wesleyan Female College in Macon, Georgia, chartered in 1836, the Troy Female Seminary of Troy, New York, established in 1821 and which turned into the Emma Willard School in 1895), Salem College, which is the oldest educational institution in North Carolina, and the thirteenth oldest college in the United States, is also, as recently documented by the American Council on Education, the oldest women's school by founding date.

When considering that North Carolina was the most culturally deprived of the colonies, the accomplishment of the Salem school founded on April 30, 1772 to provide education for the little girls of the community, is all the more to be appreciated. The University of North Carolina, the first state university in the nation, was not founded till 1789 and began operating only in 1795, on which occasion the Salem community sent its own financial contribution to Chapel Hill.

As for its present status, Salem has been named repeatedly among the nation's top 100 best schools by *Money Magazine*, a leading publication in its field, which compiles annual surveys of institutions of higher learning, evaluated in reason of their academic excellence and their financial costs. In recent years, Salem has ranked among *Money Magazine's* ten 'best buys'; and in 1994 it has been named third among women's colleges. The School of Music remains one of its major assets. Its liberal arts program is being further strengthened, while new career-oriented programs in science, medical technology, and business are being developed. Salem's scholarship and financial aid program is particularly impressive. The prestigious 'Comenius award' is given annually to friends of the college who have distinguished themselves for their service to the community.

The Salem School started with three little pupils, Maria Magdalena Schmidt, eight years old, and the little daughters of Brothers Traugott Bagge and Jacob Meyer, aged two and a half and four respectively. After 1772, it went on providing its exclusive service to the daughters of the first Moravian families in the community and in the surroundings, and then also to young girls and young women of the outer community at large, staying open through the Revolution, through the Civil War and the difficult years of the Reconstruction. Nor did it come short of its initial dedication to the care and education of young girls in the recent past when, between the 1950's and the 1980's, the great majority of women's colleges (seven out of ten) either closed or turned coeducational.

The first Salem teacher was Sister Elizabeth Osterlein who had arrived in North Carolina from Bethlehem, Pennsylvania, in October 1766 after a 29½ days strenuous trip on foot. Between 1772 and 1802 when plans were made to accept boarding students, about sixty young girls, between ages four and twelve attended the school. The subjects taught included Spelling, Reading and Writing both German and English, Arithmetic, Music and most likely Embroidery; most probably the students were also taught to memorize hymns and Bible passages. From the start the school became known for the advantages it offered to its young students. Following his visit to the Salem Community in 1791, President George Washington himself referred with interest in his diaries to the Moravian community and its girls' school.

As enrolment increased and Salem's reputation went on growing especially in the South, under Bishop Reichel the decision was made to open a boarding school and erect a new building which was completed in 1805. The first principal was Reverend Samuel Kramsch born in Silesia in 1758, an expert linguist and botanist; in addition to Samuel Kramsch's scholarly European training, the new school also benefited from his wife Susanna's acquaintance with boarding schools. Until 1949 the school continued to be headed by Moravian pastors, who usually had acquired professional teaching and administrative experience in other Moravian institutions, principally Nazareth Hall and Moravian Seminary. Salem leaders include remarkable figures in Moravian history, like, for instance, from 1806 to 1816, Abraham Steiner, known for his missionary tours among the Indians with Spangenberg and Conrad Weiser (1696-1760), who led the German Palatines to New York and Pennsylvania; from 1834 to 1844 John Christian Jacobson, born in the Duchy of Schleswig in 1795, and ordained as Bishop in 1854 (under his term the school increased to 195 boarding students and nineteen teachers) from 1848 to 1853 and from 1853 to 1866 respectively brothers Emil and Robert de Schweinitz, direct descendants of Zinzendorf, and both born in Salem. Robert, who became President of the Provincial Elders' Conference after leaving Salem, aptly guided the school through the Civil War years. Other principals were Maximilian Grunert, facing the Reconstruction financial hardships, Theophilus Zaru, Edward Rondthaler, John Clewell. Howard Rondthaler, son of Bishop Edward, took the School through four decades of expansion and growth and greatly contributed also to the growth of the Southern Province of his Church. In 1949 Dr. Dale H. Gramley became the first of Salem's Presidents to be inaugurated; a native of Pennsylvania, himself not a Moravian nor a minister, he effectively led the school until he retired in 1971.

With the inception of the boarding school in the first decade of the nineteenth century, Salem opened extensively to non-Moravians, and although the Church maintained solid control of the school itself, by 1811 when the boarding school became one with the day school, more and more students were enrolled who were of different Protestant creeds and often coming from outside North Carolina; already by 1807 German remained a requirement only for Moravian students who, from then on and to this day, were outnumbered by non-Moravians though continuing to represent, as it were, the very heart of the school – historian Adelaide Fries herself received her first academic training at Salem.

Other events in the first years of the boarding school point to the changes the Moravian community itself was beginning to undergo and which would gradually lead to its overall secularization by mid-nineteenth century as a result also of the pressures to adapt to the increasing industrialization and urbanization of American society. Until 1811, for example, the Single Sisters themselves had provided all housekeeping duties connected with the school, but as the load work kept adding, the Elders' Conference allowed the school to pay 400 dollars for Betsey, a Negro woman, to help with the washing and ironing chores.

In some special ways, the role of Salem in women's education soon went even beyond state and regional borders. Among its first boarding students, for example, was Sarah Childress, from Murfreesborough, Tennessee, who attended Salem in 1817; that year among the young men from Chapel Hill visiting Salem on 'speaking nights' was young Jim Polk whom Sarah married in 1822. As the wife of James K. Polk, who became President in 1845, Sarah Childress Polk is remembered as an austere but exemplary First Lady.[52]

Among its students, Salem also counted the daughters of Dr. Robert Morrison, the first President of Presbyterian Davidson College, which opened in 1837; the fourth of the Morrison 'clan', Mary Anna, who was at Salem from 1847 to 1849, married Thomas Jonathan Jackson in 1857. General Thomas 'Stonewall' Jackson was the greatest of Lee's lieutenants; an outstanding military tactician, after his death at the battle of Chancelorville in 1862, he was mourned by Federalists and Confederates alike.[53]

Students whose presence at Salem highlights the particular reputation of the school even among high government officials and political leaders include, for example, Belle Patterson, grand-daughter of President Andrew Johnson, who succeeded Lincoln – she was at Salem from 1873 to 1877; Alice Aycock Poe, daughter of North Carolina Governor Charles

Aycock, at Salem in 1907. Like the history of the Moravian Church in general, the history of Salem interconnects significantly – tragically at times – with that of the native American Indians of the Five Nations. In 1835 and following years, several Indian girls were enrolled at Salem, the first being Jane Ross, daughter of the Cherokee leader John Ross and Mary Stapler, who was herself educated at the Moravian Seminary of Bethlehem. Jane Ross remained at Salem until July 1838, when she left with her family to Cherokee County, Oklahoma, which was the final destination of the route that later became known as the infamous 'Trail of Tears'.[54]

In addressing students of diverse backgrounds to whom it imparted scholarly teaching and moral discipline, caring for their academic and personal enrichment, the Salem school was remaining true to the Moravian motto, borrowed from Saint Augustine, 'In essentials unity, in non-essentials liberty; in all things charity'. It is this spirit that Salem has continued to pass on unto its students to this day, despite inevitable hardships and obstacles (as well as drawbacks that may at times result from living in too small a community).

After seriously decreasing in the 1980's, Salem enrolment is presently above 900. Students represent different socio-cultural and religious backgrounds, Roman Catholics included, and so do the Faculty. All parts of the United States and other parts of the world, especially Europe, Latin America, and Asia are represented in the student body; in 1972 Alma Hines Boyd was the first Afro American woman to graduate from Salem College.

In the last years, students and Faculty alike (despite their different origins) have become more and more concerned with the Moravian legacy of which Salem itself is a part. Dr. Julienne Still Shrift, who was inaugurated the first Salem Woman President in 1992, explained with bold confidence: 'Salem is a treasure. But we are a light under a bushel, when we ought to be a city on a hilltop. We must be a beacon – alight unto all women. ... It is our challenge not just to value our history, but to make history'.[55]

Most interesting is the experience of the four students who in May 1994 have ridden their bicycles from Bethlehem to Winston-Salem, from Pennsylvania to North Carolina, across Maryland and Virginia, via Lancaster, York, Hagerstown, Winchester, Staunton, Roanoke, and Mount Airy, approximately retracing the 500 miles route covered by foot in 29 days by the first sixteen young women who reached the Wachovia settlement in 1766 and among whom was Sister Elisabeth who became Salem's first teacher. Faculty member Dr. Dudley Shearburn had first called attention to the memorable trip of the first Salem Sisters when she herself, then aged 52, covered their route on foot in May and June 1981.

As the twenty-first century is fast approaching, like the Moravian community at large, Salem faces the challenge of living in an ever-developing technological society and in an increasingly global environment. Catherine Holderness, a young Faculty member, recently commented on the installation of a new telecommunication network to improve the school's access to Internet, which is helping internationalize Salem curricula, saying: 'Telecommunications will be a vital link. We will no longer be limited by our location in historical Old Salem. Because of computers and fax machines, all barriers will be gone. We can become a college without walls – while still being steeped in a rich Moravian heritage'.[56] Her words reflect the outlook to the future which is typical of the Moravian vision at its best.

NOTES

1 J. Taylor Hamilton, 'A History of the *Unitas Fratrum*, or Moravian Church, in the United States of America' in *A History of the Reformed Churches in the United States*, E.T. Corwin ed., (New York: Scribner, 1902), pp. 433-437. The first Moravian refugees, who reached Saxony after a long journey on foot, were the families of brothers Augustin and Jacob Neisser of Sehlen, a group of ten including three infants, a three-year-old girl and twins of three months (J.T. Hamilton, p.436). See also Adelaide Fries, ed., *Records of the Moravians in North Carolina* (North Carolina Historical Commission: Raleigh, 1922), p. 13.

2 On the episcopal tradition of the *Unitas Fratrum*, see J.T. Hamilton, p. 431. Presbyterial ordination of three members of the religious group founded in 1457 was received from priests who had joined the new religious association; episcopal ordination was then received by Michael Bradacius from Bishop Steven of the Waldenses who had been ordained by bishops at the Council of Basel (this Council, which opened in 1431, was characterized by conflicts between supporters of episcopal decentralization and supporters of absolute papal authority). Missionary activity took the *Unitas Fratrum* particularly to Greenland, to Africa, to Central and North America (including Labrador and Alaska), to South America (Surinam), to Asia (Tibet), and to the Holy Land. It is argued that the Moravians' accomplishment for Protestant missions is comparable to the missionary activity of the Jesuits in the context of the Catholic Church: cf. A. Bestor, *Backwood Utopias: The Sectarian origins and the Owenite Phase of Communitarian Socialism in America, 1663-1829* (Philadelphia: University of Pennsylvania Press, 1970), p. 31. The Moravians paved the way for the great missionary expansion in the nineteenth century.

3 On the development of the Moravian Church, see in particular J. Taylor Hamilton and Kenneth Hamilton, *History of the Moravian Church: the Renewed Unitas Fratrum, 1722-1957* (Winston-Salem: Interprovincial Board of Christian Education, 1967).

4 J. Taylor Hamilton, *op. cit.*, pp. 445-446. At the time of his visit to Pennsylvania, Zinzendorf, temporarily banished from Saxony, used the cover name of Türnstein.

5 *Ibid.*, p. 398. A. Fries, ed., *op. cit.*, p. 1204 *et passim*.

6 J. Taylor Hamilton, *op. cit.*, p. 469. A. Fries, ed., *op. cit.*, p. 203. See also Weinlick, pp. 158-170 (Zinzendorf mentioned his disagreement with Whitefield's sensational preaching, referring to the Methodists as 'those mobs'.

7 On the interaction between the leaders of the *Renewed Unitas* and John Wesley (1703-1791), his brother Charles (1707-1770) and George Whitefield (1714-1770) see J. Taylor Hamilton, *John Weinlich, Count Zinzendorff: the Story of His Life and Leadership in the Renewed Moravian Church* (New York, Nashville: Abingdon Press, 1956), p. 128.

8 Arthur Bestor, *op. cit.*, pp. 20-25; in his discussion of the religious 'communitive sects', Bestor refers in particular to Ernst Troeltsch's *The Social Teaching of the Christian Churches* (English translation, London, 1931) and his definition of the seventeenth century religious sect, 'a religious association or conventicle, which aims at realizing within its own circle, as far as possible, the ideal of love and holiness'; which seeks 'to withdraw from all contacts with the State, and with force and secular power, and in a voluntary union to realize the evangelical Law of God, thus creating a society within Society'. The early Moravian settlements in Georgia, and then Pennsylvania and North Carolina fit this definition (except that the Moravian leaders were concerned with remaining on good terms with the representatives of the State); nevertheless, the Moravian communities were also since the start somehow part of a Church body: when their ties with the Lutherans were no longer effective, the Moravian leaders, who had initially seen their association as part of the Lutheran Church, especially at Zinzendorf's urge, soon insisted on conferring it ecclesiastical identity, after assuring Apostolic continuity with the ancient *Unitas Fratrum*. Bestor also indicates that the Moravians' communal system, like that of other religious and non religious utopian communities, was intensified in the New World because of the pressures of frontier existence. The communal system of the *Renewed Unitas Fratrum* in Europe, particularly at Herrnhut, lasted much longer than in the New World, as Gillian Lindt Gollin has shown in *Moravians in Two Worlds: A Study in Changing Communities* (New York: Columbia, U.P., 1967); yet, while in America the Moravian communities embodied a dynamic organization, aiming in the end at social progress, reform, and improvement (in part at least, in reason also of their experimental nature and of the diverse social extraction of the Brothers), in the Old World, on the other hand, some of the Moravian communities, like Herrnhut, were more likely to correspond to Toynbee's definition of utopias as 'arrested civilizations' quoted by Bestor (p. 3), 'the "pegging" at a certain level of a society which has entered on a decline'. Bestor's study, which is central to a discussion of separation in American culture, is also relevant to a discussion of the tradition of American pacifism and the author also recalls discussing his work in particular with Merle Curti; in his writings Merle Curti has dealt extensively with the pacifist trends in American society (see *Peace or War: the American Struggle, 1636-1936*, 1936).

9 Peter Brock, *Pacifism in the United States from the Colonial Era to the First World War* (Princeton: Princeton U.P., 1970), pp. 285-329; *Freedom From Violence: Sectarian Non-Resistance from the Middle Ages to the Great war* (Toronto: Univ. of Toronto Press), pp. 197, 269; *Pacifism in Europe to 1911* (Princeton: Princeton U.P., 1972), p. 52 (on *Unitas Fratrum* and on the European branch of the Moravian Church, Herrnhutters). Historical peace churches are represented by the Mennonites, the Quakers, and the Brethren (also known informally as the Dunkards). During the Revolution the Shakers were also known for their pacifism (Mother Ann Lee, who arrived in America in 1774, had been herself a follower of a Quaker sect in England). The Shakers, who favored celibacy, reached a membership of 6,000 in the first half of the nineteenth century; a few Shaker communities have been maintained to this day, though mostly for historic reasons. Other names for the Shakers are 'United Society of Believers in Christ's Second Coming', 'the Millennial church', the 'Children of Truth (or *Aletheians*)'. Edward Everett writing in the *North American Review* attacking the Shakers is an example of a common attitude in mid-nineteenth century. Other pacifist bodies in colonial times included the Schwenckfelders, who briefly interacted with the Moravians, and the Rogerenes. The Mennonites, the Amish and the Hutterites, representing a major radical pacifist group who migrated to North America after 1870, are all descended from sixteenth century Anabaptists.

10 See J. Taylor Hamilton, pp. 461-3, 470-2, 479-85, 499-502. Hamilton refers in particular also to G.H. Loskiel, *History of the Mission of the United Brethren among the Indians in North America* (transl. by C.I. Latrobe, London, 1794, first published in German at Barby, Saxony, in 1789), E. de Schweinitz, *The Life and Times of David Zeisberger, the Western Pioneer and Apostle of the Indians* (Philadelphia: J.B. Lippincott, 1870), A. Thompson, ed., *Transactions of the Moravian Historical Society* (Nazareth, Pa., 1859-1892). See also W.M. Beauchamps, ed., *Moravian Journals Relating to Central New York, 1745-1766* (Onandaga Historical Association, Syracuse, N.Y.: Dehler Press, 1916), with references to the tour of Brother Joseph (Spangenberg); I am most grateful to Jeanne Henriette Louis for calling my attention to this little-known Moravian source which is of particular interest as it carries also a list of Moravians who fought in the American Revolution.

11 I refer to Winston-Salem in this context in 'Utopia and Technology: The Moravian Community of Salem, North Carolina' in *Technology and the American Imagination: an Ongoing Challenge*, F. Bisutti De Riz and R. Mamoli Zorzi eds., R.S.A. vol. VII, no. 10, 1994, pp. 329-37.

12 William Mustaugh, *Moravian Architecture and Town Planning. Bethlehem, Pennsylvania and Other Eighteenth Century American Settlements* (Chapel Hill: Univ. of North Carolina P., 1967).

13 Louis Wright, *The Cultural Life of the American Colonies, 1607-1763* (New York: Harper, 1957), pp. 61, 90, 194-95. *The Autobiography of Benjamin Franklin*, 1964, pp. 230, 231, 232.

14 On Moravian schools, see in particular J. Taylor Hamilton, p. 470, and Kenneth Hamilton, pp. 48-50.

15 *Old Salem, Inc.* is a local citizens' group whose intent is to restore the Old Salem community area to its status prior to 1820. See *Salem Academy and College Alumnae Newsletter,* Winter 1993, p. 4.

16 A. Fries, *Customs and Practices of the Moravian Church* (Winston-Salem: Board of Christian Education and Evangelism, 1973).

17 Gwynne Stephen Taylor, 'Building on Our Past', *Salem,* Spring 1995, p. 9; *Salem College Bulletin,* vol. XII, no. 8, May 1970, p. 21.

18 L. Wright, p. 195.

19 Vincent G. Quinn, *Hilda Doolittle* (H.D.) (New York: Twayne, 1968).

20 In North America, the large and valuable archive collections of the Moravian Church are in Bethlehem, Pennsylvania and Winston-Salem, North Carolina. In Europe, Moravian archive centers have been in Herrnhut and Bad Boll, Germany, Prague, London, and Zeist, Holland.

21 Cf., e.g., A. Fries, *op. cit.,* pp. 23-25. J.T. Hamilton, (pp. 503-504) stresses the importance of Bishop Edmund de Schweinitz's *History of the Church Known as the Unitas Fratrum* (1885).

22 Leo Tolstoy was inspired by the work of Chelcicky, who also emphasized equal rights for women. See, for instance, Karel Stoukal, Chelcicky, Petr in *Enciclopedia Italiana, op. cit.,* vol. IX, p. 960. For useful information and bibliography on the ancient *Unitas Fratrum,* see F.M. Bartos, 'Boemi, Fratelli' in *Enciclopedia Italiana,* vol. VII, pp. 251-253.

23 Other most important personalities in the history of the *Unitas Fratrum* are Lawrence of Krasonice (Vavrinec Krasonicky, d. 1532), and later John Augusta (1500-1572).

24 Cf. P. Brock, *Pacifism in Europe, op. cit.,* pp. 44-56. See also J.T. Hamilton, pp. 432, 433. In 1619, at the eve of the Protestant defeat at the White Mountain, the candidate of the *Unitas Fratrum,* Calvinist Frederick Palatinus, was on the throne of Bohemia. On the *Renewed Unitas Fratrum* and the Lutheran and Reformed (Calvinist) Churches in Pennsylvania, see J.T. Hamilton, *op. cit.,* pp. 445, 449.

25 Cf. H.G. Good and J.D. Teller, *A History of Western Education,* (New York: McMillan), and G. Calò, 'Komensky, Jan Amos (Comenius)' in *Enciclopedia Italiana, op. cit.,* vol. XX, pp. 248-250 (1933).

26 J.T. Hamilton, *op. cit.,* p. 439.

27 Zinzendorf was godson of Philip Jakob Spener, the very initiator of the Pietist movement.

28 See J.T. Hamilton, *op. cit.,* p. 443. Zinzendorf took orders as a Lutheran pastor in 1734; he was consecrated Bishop of the *Renewed Unitas Fratrum* in 1737, and in 1743 he became the chief representative of the *Unitas.* He was banished from Saxony from 1736 to 1746.

29 J.T. Hamilton, *op. cit.,* p. 439.

30 *Ibid.,* p. 440, no. 2, 3.

31 A. Fries ed., *op. cit.,* pp. 353, 356, 753, 841, 184.

32 *Ibid.,* p. 84.

33 J.T. Hamilton, *op. cit.,* pp. 454-455; A. Fries ed., *op. cit.,* p. 1012.

34 *Ibid.,* p. 454; compare Hamilton's definition of the Moravian community, 'a sort of Christian Republic in miniature' with Bestor's discussion of Moravian religious communities in the context of utopian communal living. Note also

Hamilton's reference to the Dunkards (Brethren) of Conrad Beissel, the 'Protestant monks and nuns' of Ephrata as part of 'all sorts of religious excrescences' (p. 444).

35 Entries in the Moravian Records edited by A.Fries such as 'Andreas Betz left' for 1767, or the one for 1769 concerning two boys who had run away to work on a farm, indicate instances of resistance to the discipline and demands of community life.

36 J.T. Hamilton, *op. cit.*, p. 454.

37 Sugar cake and Moravian cookies of German origin are part of the Salem tradition, like pottery and other handicrafts. Special religious practices in the early communities included the use of the lot (which was restricted in mid-nineteenth century) and the washing of the feet on given occasions.

38 J.T. Hamilton, *op. cit.*, pp. 487, 470.

39 I discuss this and other issues related to Moravian pacifism in E. Marras, 'Amidst War and Peace: The Pacifist Identity of the Moravian Communities in North America in the Eighteenth Century', Proceedings of the 12th Biennial Meeting of the Italian Association for North American Studies (AISNA), Rome, October 1995 (forthcoming).

40 A. Fries ed., *op. cit.*

41 The ban on military service was withdrawn in Pennsylvania in 1818, in North Carolina in 1831.

42 A. Fries ed., *op. cit.*, p. 24.

43 J.T. Hamilton, p. 473. See also P. Brock, 'The Peace Testimony of the Early American Moravians: An Ambiguous Witness' in *Pacifism in the United States, op. cit.*, pp. 303-309. Strict observance of pacifism seen as a fundamental aspect of the Church's heritage depended to a large degree on the attitude of individual community leaders; Brother Matthew Hell, of Lititz, for example, was known for firmly encouraging adherence to non-combatancy; on the other hand, see also Brock (p. 309) on William Henry (1729-1788), who had joined the Moravians in 1765 and then became an officer in the Revolutionary army.

44 P. Brock calls attention to this aspect of Moravian pacifism in *Pacifism in the United States*, p. 313.

45 See Michael Shirley, 'Yeoman Culture and Millworker Protest in Antebellum Salem, North Carolina', *Journal of Southern History*, LVIII, 3 (August 1991), pp. 427-452.

46 J.T. Hamilton, pp. 480, 484.

47 Bethlehem had a population of about 140 in 1740; Salem counted about 75 adults in 1770 (cf. A. Fries, *op. cit.*, p. 356). In 1748 Moravian Indians were 500 approximately.

48 Starting in the sixteenth century, in the Christian world the 'missionary', who learns the language of the people among whom he is active, replaced the 'pilgrim' and the 'crusader', and acquired a special role as an institutionalized cultural intermediary, as shown particularly in studies occasioned by the Quincentennial of Columbus' first Ocean crossing; see A. Prosperi, 'Dal Cristianesimo mediterraneo al cristianesimo atlantico: sulle origini della idea di missione', Tradizione e Innovazione nell'America moderna, Meeting of the Association of European Historians (ASE), Ibiza, 21-24 October 1992; B. Escandell Bonet, 'Un Planteamento fenomenologico: la accion misionera

balear en Indias' in *Teoria del discurso historiografico*, Servicio de Publicaciones Universidad de Oviedo, 1992, pp. 257-283. J.T. Hamilton (pp. 462, 484-86) indicates the extent to which the missionaries' efforts were suddenly destroyed by state government policies aiming at gaining control of Indian lands when the federal authority did not intervene to check 'the rapa-city of Georgia' (p. 49). In their early tours among the Indians, the Moravians relied on expert guides, like Madame de Montour (who, however, was apparently hostile to Zinzendorf), or Conrad Weisser, the government agent, as well as on Indian interpreters. Moravians were also active among the black slaves, particularly in South and North Carolina.

49 A. Fries ed., *op. cit.*, pp. 87, 197.

50 Prior to 1807, when the Theological Seminary started operating at Nazareth, all Moravian ministers were trained in Europe. In mid-nineteenth century, the Moravians were active among the German and Scandinavian (mostly Norwegian) communities in the Northwest and in New York city. See J.T. Hamilton, pp. 492, 497. In addition to publications in English (e.g. *The Moravian*, founded in 1859) the Church printing offices also started issuing German publications, the *Bruderblatt*, Philadelphia, 1854-1866), the weekly *Der Bruder Botschafter* (Bethlehem, 1866-1893), the illustrated children's paper *Der Mission Freund* (Bethlehem, 1867) corresponding to the English *The Little Missionary*.

51 Cited in *Rondthaler Circle*, Salem, vol. XXII, no. 7, p. 4 (originally in a story by Chester Davis in the July 3, 1949 issue of *The Winston-Salem Journal and Sentinel*. Information on Salem College is taken from *Salem College Bulletin*, vol. XII, no. 8, (May 1970), pp. 6-37; vol. XIV, no. 6 (March 1972); vol. XXII, no. 3 (June 1980); vol. XXIV, no. 3 (December 1981); *Salem Quarterly*, vol. 33, no. 2, *The Salem Newsletter*, 1990; *Salem College Alumnae Magazine*, August 1992, August 1993, Spring 1994, Winter 1994, Summer 1994, Summer 1995. See also Frances Griffin, *Less Time for Meddling. A History of Salem Academy and College, 1772-1866* (J. Blair Publisher, 1981); the 1866 date, which relates to the historical period corresponding to the time when the Civil War period was over, is also the year in which the State of North Carolina incorporated the Salem School. Griffin indicates that the only girls' school of any consequence in the South was the Ursuline Convent in New Orleans. Salem School archive documents are in English.

52 Before attending the University of North Carolina, James Polk (1795-1849), a native of North Carolina, attended the academy of Murfreesboro, Tennessee; he is remembered as probably the hardest working of all American Presidents. With her irreproachable behavior Sarah Childress Polk was noted for banning cards and dancing from the White House.

53 Mary Anna Morrison Jackson's sisters were also related to Confederate leaders. Mary Anna Morrison Jackson was awarded an honorary Bachelor of Arts degree by Salem College in 1915.

54 See J.T. Hamilton, p. 499 on 'Chief John Ross, or Kroweskowee', the head of the Cherokee nation, 'a well-educated Christian gentleman, and attached to the Moravian Church by various ties'. Ross (who was one-eighth Cherokee) had headed a Cherokee regiment under General Andrew Jackson in 1812. As the leader of his nation, he strongly resisted orders for the Cherokee to vacate

their Georgia lands, when gold was found there, and even brought his people's
case to the Supreme Court in 'Cherokee vs. Georgia' in 1831, but Jackson
and the Supreme Court ruled against the rights of the Indian nation. Moravian
and other Protestant missionaries pointed out the injustice of official policy
in this instance. Threatened with military force, in 1838, Ross consented to
lead 17,000 Cherokees West to Oklahoma.

55 *Salem*, August 1993, p. 7. President Thrift stresses the advantages of women's
schools which allow young women better to develop their potential leadership
and learn to become competitive.

56 *Salem*, Winter 1994, p. 12.

Selected Index